Then & Now

of Stark County

by Harold R. Thomas

This publication accompanies an exhibit of the same name at the Canton Museum of Art, May 1 - August 14, 2005 celebrating Canton's Bicentennial.

Published by JnR Photographic Services.
    Canton, Ohio
    330-452-6581

Design by David Bissett.

Maps by Harold D. Thomas.

Printing by Lowry Lithograph Company.

ISBN 0-9766255-0-4

CONTENTS

MAPS

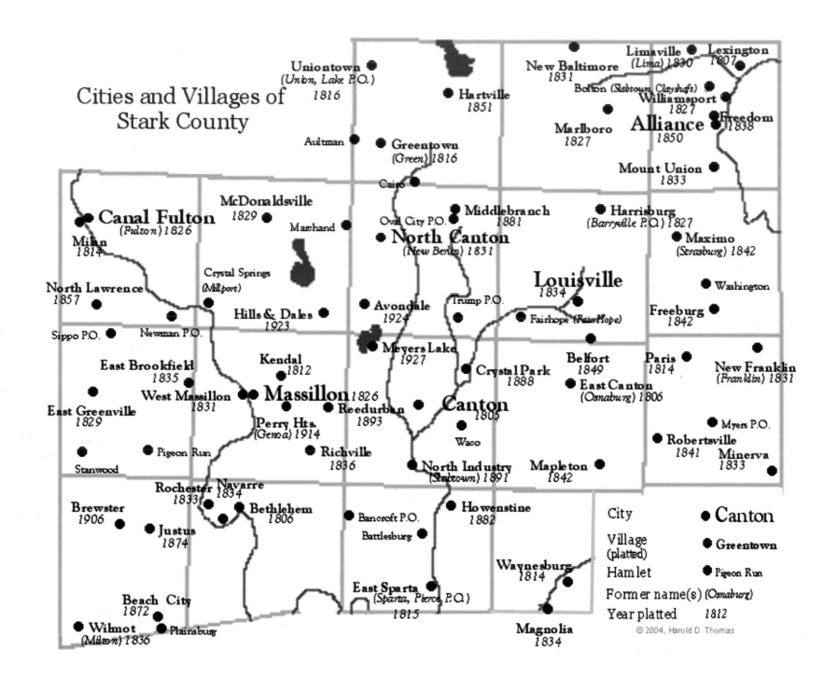

Cities and Villages of Stark County

Uniontown (Union, Lake P.O.) 1816
Hartville 1851
New Baltimore 1831
Limaville (Lima) 1830
Lexington 1807
Bolton (Slabtown, Clayshaft)
Williamsport 1827
Freedom 1838
Marlboro 1827
Alliance 1850
Aultman
Greentown (Green) 1816
Mount Union 1833
Cairo
McDonaldsville 1829
Marchand
Oval City P.O.
Middlebranch 1881
Harrisburg (Barrville P.O.) 1827
Canal Fulton (Fulton) 1826
North Canton (New Berlin) 1831
Maximo (Strasburg) 1842
Milan 1814
Crystal Springs (Millport)
Louisville 1834
Washington
North Lawrence 1857
Hills & Dales 1923
Avondale 1924
Trump P.O.
Freeburg 1842
Sippo P.O.
Newman P.O.
Fairhope (Fair Hope)
Meyers Lake 1927
East Brookfield 1835
Kendal 1812
Belfort 1849
Paris 1814
New Franklin (Franklin) 1831
West Massillon 1831
Massillon 1826
Crystal Park 1888
East Canton (Osnaburg) 1806
East Greenville 1829
Reedurban 1893
Canton 1805
Perry Hts. (Genoa) 1914
Waco
Myers P.O.
Pigeon Run
Richville 1836
Robertsville 1841
Stanwood
North Industry (Slabtown) 1891
Mapleton 1842
Minerva 1833
Rochester 1833
Navarre 1834
Brewster 1906
Bethlehem 1806
Howenstine 1882
Justus 1874
Bancroft P.O.
Battlesburg
Waynesburg 1814
Beach City 1872
East Sparta (Sparta, Pierce P.O.) 1815
Wilmot (Milton) 1836
Plainsburg
Magnolia 1834

City — Canton
Village (platted) — Greentown
Hamlet — Pigeon Run
Former name(s) (Osnaburg)
Year platted 1812

© 2004, Harold D. Thomas

4

INTRODUCTION
by Harold D. Thomas

"Nothing endures but change." – HERACLITUS (c. 540-c. 480 BC)

Change is the reason that history exists. By comparing the present with the past, we learn how our environment, our politics, our social life, and even our values have become what they are today.

This is the appeal of *Then & Now.* We see in its pictures how our forebears turned a forest wilderness into farms, canals, cities, factories, schools, highways, railroads, quarries, electrical transmission lines, city homes, country estates, and suburban sprawl. We learn what they and we found important enough to keep, and what was thrown away. We can thus more clearly understand what we did right and what mistakes we made; and we can gain a clearer vision of the Stark County we want to leave for our descendants.

The purpose of this introduction is not to give a complete history of Stark County. Those who desire a detailed account should consult the works cited in the Bibliography, along with the many city, village, township, and corporate histories available in the public libraries and at the Wm. McKinley Presidential Library and Museum. Still, a bit of context may help the reader enjoy the drawings and photographs that follow.

Stark County history may be thought of as consisting of seven eras, each with distinct events and themes. If we were to give each a single descriptive term, they might be: Prehistoric, Frontier, Canal, Railroad, Manufacturing, Progress, and Transition.

PREHISTORIC (before 1761)

Stark County has an area of 567 square miles, most of which was heavily forested; except for plains over the western half of the city of Canton, and the townships of Plain, Canton, and Perry. Elevation ranges from 880 feet in the southeast corner of Bethlehem Township, to 1,360 feet on a hill north of Paris. The glacier that covered much of North America about 20,000 years ago ended along a line running through the middle of the county. The soil throughout the county is excellent for farming. Of particular note is the swamp land in Lake and Marlboro Townships, which is widely known for cultivating onions, radishes, and celery. The soils produced have been beneficial for industry as well as agriculture: the county has an abundance of gravel, limestone, sandstone, and clay.

The earliest settlers in what is now Stark County were mound builders, probably of the Hopewell culture, though only two mounds are known in the county, the better known of which is one on the Yant farm in southeastern Bethlehem Township, 60 feet in diameter, standing about six feet above a level field in a low tract of land. Prior to 1750, no tribes lived permanently in the area. After 1750, some Delaware established a capital at Tuscarawastown (near Bolivar in Tuscarawas County). The only known Indian battle was a minor brush with Federal troops near Waynesburg in 1793. Most of the Indians residing in Stark County left following the War of 1812, although a few bands could be found as late as 1825.

FRONTIER (1761-1825)

The first known European settler in Ohio was a Moravian missionary, Christian Frederick Post, who lived for two years in a cabin he built on the Tuscarawas in Bethlehem Township in 1761. In 1785, the Continental Congress passed the Land Ordinance, which ordered surveys in the Congress Lands of eastern Ohio, dividing it into sections one mile square. Three other events facilitated settlement: the Ordinance of 1787, providing the Northwest Territory with a legal foundation; the Treaty of Greenville in 1795, which opened to settlement most of Ohio, including all of Stark County east of the Tuscarawas River; and Ohio's statehood in 1803. Stark and Wayne Counties were part of an unorganized area until Columbiana County was created in 1803. The maps in this section display the changes in county and township boundaries that have affected Stark County since then.

Bezaleel Wells, a state senator from Jefferson County and founder of Steubenville, learned that the lands west of the Tuscarawas River would be opened to white settlement on July 4, 1805, and that a road would be run connecting Lisbon with Wooster. While traveling through the forest, he found a clearing at the confluence of the West and East Branches of Nimishillen Creek, which would provide him with a considerable advantage over developers of other towns in the area. With this in mind, he purchased 10 square miles at $2.00 per acre and laid which became the county seat when Stark County was formed in March 1809. The county was named for General John Stark, the oldest surviving general of the Revolutionary War at the time.

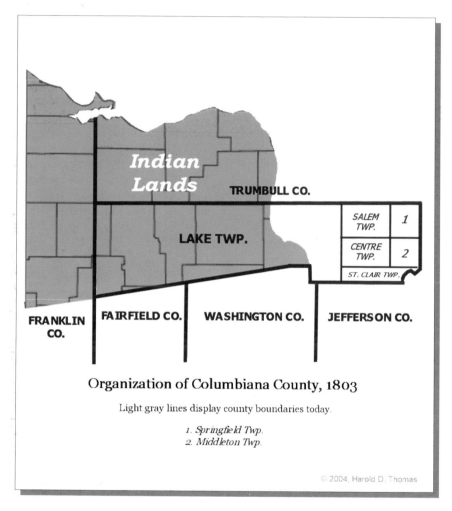

Organization of Columbiana County, 1803

Light gray lines display county boundaries today.

1. *Springfield Twp.*
2. *Middleton Twp.*

© 2004, Harold D. Thomas

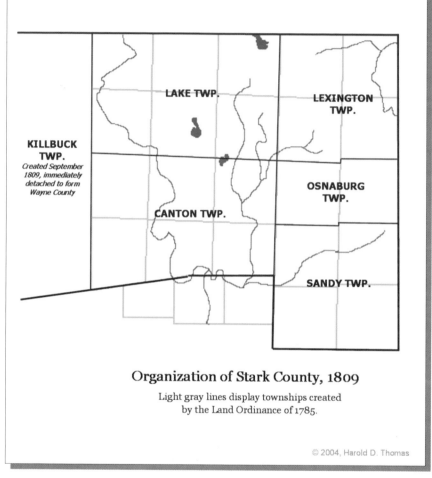

Organization of Stark County, 1809

Light gray lines display townships created
by the Land Ordinance of 1785.

© 2004, Harold D. Thomas

Between 1805 and 1816, ten villages were laid out. They served as local commercial centers for the surrounding rural areas, with tanners, blacksmith shops, grist mills, sawmills, the general store, and perhaps a saloon. Some towns also had foundries, which made cookware or simple farm implements. A few towns had flour mills; and Kendal (now part of Massillon) sported a woolen mill.

Early settlers were mostly of German extraction from Pennsylvania ("Pennsylvania Dutch"), but some settlers of English descent came to the area, principally from Maryland and Virginia. The early German settlers were Lutheran and Reformed, the English Methodist and Presbyterian. Some French settlers moved into Nimishillen Township, and established the St. Louis Roman Catholic parish in Louisville.

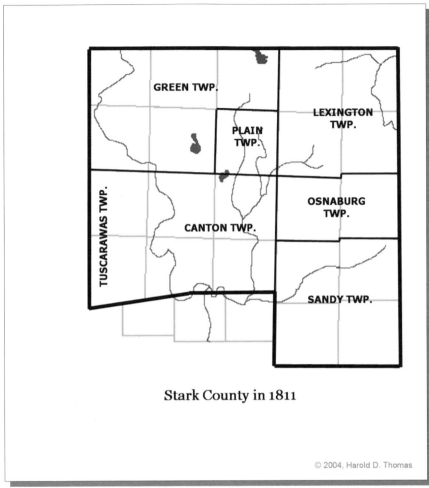

Stark County in 1811

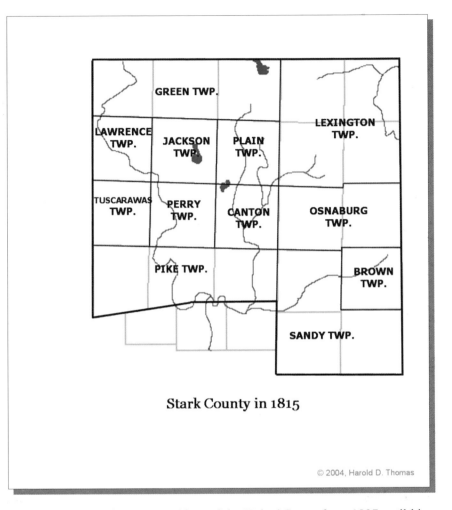

Stark County in 1815

The first known schoolhouse in Stark County was built in 1807 in Canton Township. It was made of round logs, seven feet high, with a clapboard roof. Windows were made of small logs and greased paper. Logs covered with boards formed the writing desks.

On March 30, 1815, John Saxton, a printer, established in Canton what is now the oldest newspaper west of the Appalachians still being published, originally known as the *Ohio Repository*. His granddaughter Ida married Wil-

liam McKinley, who was President of the United States from 1897 until his assassination in 1901.

CANAL (1825-1850)

In 1825 the State of Ohio began construction of the Ohio-Erie Canal linking Cleveland with Portsmouth. Canals enabled farmers to get products to market with greater efficiency, and reduced the cost of shipping provisions and

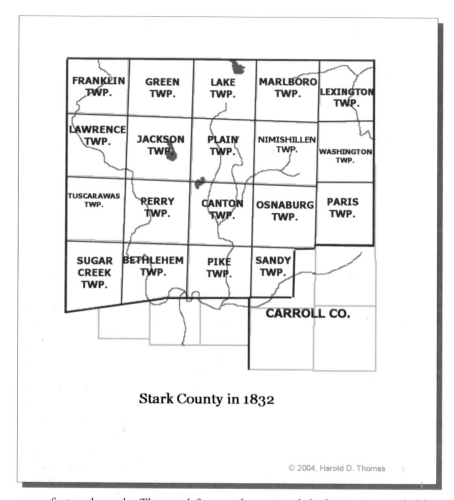

FRANKLIN TWP. | GREEN TWP. | LAKE TWP. | MARLBORO TWP. | LEXINGTON TWP.

LAWRENCE TWP. | JACKSON TWP. | PLAIN TWP. | NIMISHILLEN TWP. | WASHINGTON TWP.

TUSCARAWAS TWP. | PERRY TWP. | CANTON TWP. | OSNABURG TWP. | PARIS TWP.

SUGAR CREEK TWP. | BETHLEHEM TWP. | PIKE TWP. | SANDY TWP.

CARROLL CO.

Stark County in 1832

Ohio Northern University, and scientist Thomas Crown Mendenhall, for whom an Alaska glacier is named.

Recognizing the importance of agriculture, the Stark County Agricultural Society was formed, staging the first county fair October 15-16, 1850. The first fair was held near Second Steet and McKinley Avenue in Canton. Two years later, the fair moved to Cook Park in northeast Canton, finally settling at its present site in 1894.

RAILROAD (1850-1896)

The railroad centralized the development of heavy industry in Massillon and Canton, but dashed the hopes of the villages. It was also responsible for creating Alliance. Mathias Hester, who had founded Freedom in 1838, knew that two railroads linking Pittsburgh and Cleveland were going to cross nearby, so on September 26, 1850, he laid out the village of Alliance at that junction. The construction of shops for the Wheeling & Lake Erie Railway spurred the development of Brewster. Aultman, Beach City, Justus, and Middlebranch were also products of the railroads.

As the map on page 4 shows, many communities were founded under different names than those by which they are now known. The old Stark County atlases display hamlets with post offices that no longer exist. Today's Alliance, Beach City, Canal Fulton, Massillon, and Navarre are mergers of earlier communities.

Contrary to popular belief, "The War of the Rebellion" was actually quite controversial in Stark County. Considerable sentiment favored the Peace Democrats, or Copperheads, who opposed prosecuting the war against the South. The county also had one of the state's highest percentages of drafted men, having failed to meet its quota of enlistments. The lack of enthusiasm expressed at the beginning the war, however, was more than compensated for by the communities' pride in the Union victory after the war. For over a generation afterward, lengthy parades and lavish banquets honored the Grand Army of the Republic, a veterans' organization. Massillon sent eighteen African-American volunteers for the Fifth Infantry, the only area in Stark County to do so. Women throughout the county organized Ladies' Aid Societies to ensure that soldiers were given adequate clothing and food, and that their families did not suffer in their absence. One interesting fact is that prior to the Civil War, Christmas was little observed. It began to take hold when the desire to remember the boys in service led to the exchange of

manufactured goods. The need for warehouses and docks to store and ship products resulted in the organization of Canal Fulton, Massillon, and Navarre. By 1850, Massillon had a larger population than Canton, and for a short time pressure built for moving the county seat there. Canton compensated by being a well-established stagecoach stop. Massillon organized the "Union School," the first graded public school in Ohio, in 1847. In 1846, Oliver Hartshorn organized a school that became Mount Union College in Alliance. Marlboro, settled largely by well-educated Quaker farmers, became a seat of learning, which had an academy that drew students from afar with distinguished professors, among them Henry S. Lehr, the founder of gifts. According to a tradition, Salmon P. Chase was notified by President Lincoln of his appointment to the Supreme Court while delivering the dedication address for Chapman Hall at Mount Union College. That college also enlisted some 1,060 men in the Civil War.

Jacob Coxey won national notoriety when he organized a march from Massillon to Washington, D.C. in support of a plan to reduce unemployment by building roads. Four thousand demonstrators, dubbed "Coxey's Army," converged on the Capitol May 1, 1894, but Coxey failed to persuade the Congress. He organized another assault in 1914, which also failed; but his efforts were rewarded with his election in 1931 to a single term as Massillon's mayor.

After the war, cultural life in the three cities centered around their opera houses. In Canton, Louis Schaefer initially faced religious opposition, but his connections in the entertainment world and willingness to make the opera house available to church groups for benefits and festivals, won him the acceptance he needed. Bucher's Opera House in Massillon was an architectural gem, built in 1870 at a cost of nearly $100,000. It was considered the best opera house between Pittsburgh and Chicago. E. Crew's opera house in Alliance is best remembered for the way the structure collapsed in 1886, fortunately with enough warning to avoid fatalities. The villages also had cultural events built around their schools and through traveling lectures, plays, and concerts.

By Cornelius Aultman's death in 1884, the focus of the agricultural machinery industry had moved to Chicago; but Canton found new industries to sustain it, the best known of which were Diebold Safe & Lock, Belden Brick, and the Dueber-Hampden Watch Works. Morgan Engineering and Solid Steel Company (later part of American Steel Foundries) were established in Alliance, while in Massillon became a center for manufacturing castings for the glass-blowing industry. Canton was an early adopter of electricity for street lighting, incorporating the Canton Electric Light & Power Company in late 1883, only fifteen months after Thomas Edison completed the first central electric light station in New York. One reason might be the city's connections with Edison through his marriage to Mina Miller, daughter of Cornelius Aultman's partner Lewis Miller.

The cities began building separate high schools, and many villages moved from one-room schoolhouses to two- and four-room schools, including a high school. In the rural areas, one-room schoolhouses continued for many years.

The last to close was Science Hill, in Lexington Township, in 1952. The building is owned by the Marlington Local School District, and stands as a museum. During this period, the cities established their public libraries. Canton's began in 1884 as a room in City Hall, but, like many other American cities, expanded to a building with the help of industrialist Andrew Carnegie. A few years later, Alliance industrialist Thomas Morgan took a trip to New York to buy books for the school library, which evolved into that city's public library. Massillon's library, established in 1897, today doubles as a fine museum. The interurban railway connected Canton with Massillon and Cleveland. Brick replaced dirt and gravel as the preferred method for paving streets in the cities. With all of this excitement, it should not be surprising that the population shift at the end of the Nineteenth Century was from rural areas to urban ones.

MANUFACTURING (1896-1954)

As the Nineteenth Century turned into the Twentieth, William McKinley, who moved to Canton as a young man after the Civil War, was elected President of the United States. His economic policy, focusing on protection from foreign imports and stability in the value of the dollar, were popular with industrialist and workingman alike. He conducted his Presidential campaigns from his home (where the Stark County District Library is now located), attracting delegations from throughout the nation. One contemporary said of the time, "Every day was circus day in Canton." President McKinley felt and practiced a deep religious faith, reflected in his personal kindness and in his reluctance to engage in the Spanish-American War. His assassination in 1901 led to an outpouring of grief at a huge state funeral in Canton, which led to the construction of the McKinley Monument a few years later. President McKinley's Secretary of State was William R. Day, who founded the law firm now known as Day, Ketterer. In 1903, Day was elevated to the Supreme Court of the United States. Other notable people of the period include Massillon native Robert P. Skinner, whose diplomatic career culminated in a 1933 appointment as Ambassador to Turkey; and Canton resident Atlee Pomerene, whose brilliant legal career led him to election as Stark County Prosecutor, Lieutenant Governor, and in 1913, United States Senator.

Stark County was bustling with manufacturing activity. Histories published at this time listed every manufacturer and boasted of their accomplishments. Foremost among them is the Timken Roller Bearing Company, which began when founder H.H. Timken moved to Canton from St. Louis in 1901. Canton also became the home of Union Metal, a manufacturer of light fixtures;

Berger Steel (later Republic Steel and LTV Steel), which made sheet steel and steel products; Danner Press, a printer of mass-market publications, Belden Brick, E.W. Bliss Company, a manufacturer of signal systems; Canton Drop Forging & Manufacturing Company; the Climalene Company, which developed a line of products to soften Canton's hard water; Hercules Motors Corporation; Luntz Iron & Steel Company; Irwin Steel; Weber Dental Manufacturing Company; and Ekco Products, which made small housewares. Unfortunately, not all of the profits went into the hands of legitimate businesses. Organized crime competed for the illegal gambling franchise in Canton. Efforts to expose this activity by the *Canton Daily News* led to the assassination of its editor, Don Mellett, at his home in 1926.

Alliance became the home of Morgan Engineering, a producer of steel castings for railroad use; the Reeves boiler works, which in 1940 was purchased by Babcock & Wilcox; Alliance Manufacturing, a pioneer in development of fractional horsepower electrical motors; and Transue & Williams, which produced forgings for the automotive industry. Lamborn Floral in Alliance, had greenhouses making it a major floral wholesaler in northeast Ohio. Its founder, William Lamborn, once opposed William McKinley for Congress. Following a debate, he gave McKinley a scarlet carnation, which led to it eventually becoming the state flower of Ohio.

Massillon was home to the Hess-Snyder Company, a manufacturer of stoves; Reliance Manufacturing Company, which began by manufacturing lock washers; the Massillon Steel Casting Company; and the Central Steel Company. Benjamin Fairless, a native of Justus, began his career at Central Steel and eventually became president of United States Steel.

North Canton developed its own industry when the Hoover family, realizing that its horse-collar business would not long survive the automobile, purchased the patent for the electric suction sweeper, the first (and best known) of many appliances to be manufactured under the Hoover name.

Davis A. Cable organized the United States Quarry Tile Company in East Sparta in 1926, which gained a national reputation for its artistic tile murals; and Swiss baker Alfred Nickles established a bakery in Navarre, which has supplied bakery products throughout Ohio and in surrounding states. The Ohio Power Company (now part of AEP), through careful planning, was able to supply the growing electrical needs of Stark County industry.

Two automobile makes were manufactured in Stark County: the Jewel in Massillon in 1905-1906; and the Holmes in Canton in 1919-1921. The Holmes was expensive compared to Detroit's, since it was not made by assembly-line methods. For a time, Ford manufactured parts for automobiles that were assembled in Canton. The school safety patrols, which protect children on their way to and from school, were first organized by Harry Staley at Worley School in Canton.

The Ohio Aero Club developed an international reputation for a series of 46 balloon flights made between 1907 and 1910. Canton's Frank P. Lahm, grandson of Canton's Congressman Samuel Lahm, trained under Orville Wright and became one of the first two army pilots in the world in 1907. William H. Martin developed the first single-winged aircraft, which flew when towed by a horse or an automobile. Unfortunately, he was unable to finance installation of a motor for it. In the field of communications, radio station WHBC (for "We Help Boost Canton") began as a Christian ministry in 1925.

Modern high school buildings were constructed in Massillon (1914) and Canton (McKinley High School, 1918), which became the epicenters of a high school football rivalry that continues to attract national attention. Paul Brown Tiger Stadium and Fawcett Stadium are two of the largest high school stadiums in the nation, each with a capacity exceeding 20,000 spectators. The opera houses in Canton were replaced in 1904 by an Auditorium that at the time was the fourth largest such facility in the nation.

Cultural activities included dramatic and literary (or debating) societies. The cities and many of the villages had community bands and local amateur football teams. Two of them, the Canton Bulldogs and the Massillon Tigers became professional teams. Jim Thorpe, player-owner of the Bulldogs, spearheaded the organization of the National Football League in 1920 in a Canton automobile showroom. Athletics were also represented by the growth of the Young Men's Christian Association (YMCA) in the cities, and in Canton by the *Turnvereins* (gymnastics clubs), which along with singing societies, were distinctive features of German-American life. Canton also had professional baseball teams, including the Terriers in the 1930s, and the Indians and Crocodiles in the 70s and 80s. New York Yankees catcher Thurman Munson was a Canton resident. Other noted sports figures include Massillon's National Football League star Chris Spielman, and North Canton's Dick Snyder, who played in the National Basketball Association. In 1955, four Stark County men were drafted by National Football League teams.

Major flooding throughout Ohio in 1913 led to systems of dams, levees, and artificial lakes in the Muskingum Watershed Conservancy District, completed in 1937; and the Massillon Conservancy District, a much smaller but very complex project, in 1952. In October 1918, Canton suffered from a deadly outbreak of Spanish flu, which claimed 473 lives, compared with only 119 soldiers killed in World War I. The next decade saw the construction of modern buildings at Aultman and Mercy Hospitals, and of Molly Stark Hospital, which began as a tuberculosis facility. After the war, suburban development began to reverse the earlier migration into the cities. Developers built Avondale, Hills & Dales, and a number of golf courses throughout the county.

Between 1925 and 1940, the 170 district schools were consolidated into a smaller number of local school districts. The Stark County School District initiated a program that led to new school buildings throughout the villages and rural areas of the county. A $1.25 million gift from the Timken foundation led to the construction of Timken Vocational High School in 1939, one of the first schools in the state to concentrate on providing training for the trades in addition to basic academics. Massillon built three junior high schools between 1921 and 1939, among the first of their kind in Ohio.

Culturally, the Canton and Massillon Women's Clubs were established, along with garden clubs in several communities. Men's service clubs, such as the Rotary, Kiwanis, and Lions Clubs, sprouted throughout the county. Canton's cultural institutions were all organized in the 1930s, including the Canton Museum of Art, the Player's Guild, the Canton Symphony Orchestra, and the Canton Civic Opera. Harry Ink built Canton's Palace Theatre in 1926, bringing sound motion pictures to Canton. The old Canton Auditorium, condemned in 1941, was replaced in 1952 by the Canton Memorial Auditorium, which anchors the Cultural Center for the Arts on the old Harter Estate north of downtown Canton. The Timken Foundation provided funding for the Cultural Center, which houses the Canton Museum of Art and the Players Guild.

A discussion of the educational and cultural life in Stark County would not be complete without reference to Edward Thornton Heald's massive six-volume history, *The Stark County Story,* begun as scripts for a weekly radio program and completed in 1959. Heald wrote several other books, including a biography of William McKinley, and a one-volume abridgement of *The Stark County Story.*

As with the rest of the country, World War II forced Stark County to focus its energies on winning the war; so much so in Massillon that the city received the Army and Navy Salute for having virtually 100% of its industrial production directed to the war effort. The city was also believed to have the highest percentage in the nation of its population engaged in the war effort. Many firms throughout the county won the Army-Navy "E" for effort awards for outstanding production. To promote civil aviation as a wartime defense measure, the county commissioners of Stark and Summit Counties organized the construction of Akron-Canton Airport in Green, which opened for its first flight in July 1948.

PROGRESS (1954-1982)

During the postwar period, suburbs grew outward from the cities. Much of the growth occurred in Louisville and North Canton, which in 1960 became cities themselves. By 1958, Canton had four shopping centers, beginning with Country Fair at West Tuscarawas Street and Whipple Avenue. Amherst Park in Massillon and College Plaza in Alliance were also constructed at this time. The first shopping mall was Belden Village, built in 1970. In 1956, Canton voters decided to build the Canton Expressway, which was connected to Interstate 77 in 1966. Sadly, construction of the Expressway necessitated the destruction of the beautiful, wooded Ink Park, which linked Canton's inner city parks to Arboretum Park, north of 38th Street.

At the end of World War II, Canton was the largest city in the United States without a college, a situation rectified in the 1950s with the development of Kent State University's Stark County branch and Malone College. Walsh College built a campus east of North Canton in 1959; and Mt. Union College in Alliance undertook a major building campaign. Stark County Technical Institute began in 1959 on Frank Road in Jackson Township. The six cities and Minerva maintained public library systems with combined book circulation over 2.2 million in 1960. The Stark County Historical Society (now the William McKinley Presidential Library and Museum) constructed its present facility in 1963.

Canton also began to clean up its downtown under the leadership of young Safety Director Stanley A. Cmich in 1953. His efforts, along with those of the Citizens Committee for Good Government, led to Canton receiving the National Municipal League's All-American City award that year. In 1963, he would begin a twenty-year tenure as mayor of Canton. The old City Hall and fire station were razed to make room for Canton's distinctive glass and steel structure, dedicated in 1961. The following year saw the construction of

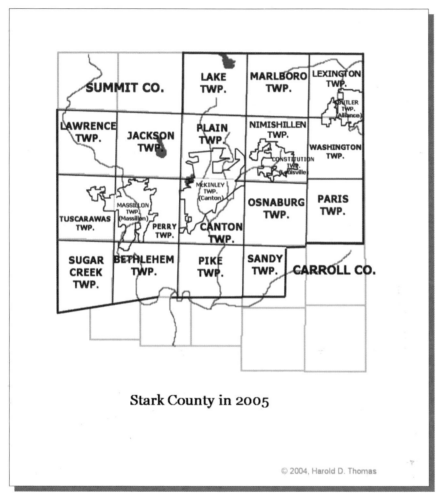

Stark County in 2005

© 2004, Harold D. Thomas

the Professional Football Hall of Fame, and the beginning of Canton's annual weeklong festival that attracts visitors from throughout the world.

Many villages boasted their own high schools, which became powers in Class B athletics, but which came to an end in the statewide consolidation of small school districts in 1956-1958, resulting in the city and local school districts that appear today. In 1957, Greentown became the first unincorporated village to set up its own park.

TRANSITION (1982–)

The closure of Youngstown Sheet & Tube in 1982 began a series of plant closings and layoffs that had a devastating effect on Stark County's economy, as manufacturing plants and jobs moved from Stark County, usually to Mexico and other countries. In the 1990s, local governments and chambers of commerce tried with some success to compensate by creating an environment friendly to the growth of small manufacturing and distribution firms.

The political composition of the county in the late 20th Century turned Stark into a swing county (in a traditionally swing state), which displayed a strong tendency to support the candidate who ultimately won. As a result, it gained considerable national media attention in the Presidential campaigns.

Massillon began an ambitious downtown redevelopment in the Lowrey-Price area in 1984, followed by a similar project in Canton in the 1990s. During the 1990s, suburban growth exploded in Lake, Jackson, Plain, Nimishillen, and Tuscarawas townships, matched by a continued decline in the populations of Canton and Alliance, which Massillon avoided through an aggressive program of annexation. Through an effort spearheaded by Suzanne Timken and Mary Regula, wife of long-term Congressman Ralph Regula, the childhood home of First Lady Ida Saxton McKinley was restored to become the national First Ladies Library in 1997.

ABOUT THIS BOOK
Then & Now began in 1966, when Harold R. Thomas purchased half interest in Canton Art & Photo Service (now JnR Photographic Services). Since one of the firm's specialties is the restoration of black and white photographs, he obtained permission from their owners to make copy negatives of those he considered to be of historical interest. In the last two years, he has contacted local industries, historical societies, and interested individuals to obtain the collection of more than 550 historical photographs found in this book. At the same time, he has returned to the original locations to shoot the "Now" photo.

The reader may note that there are few portraits of individuals, and relatively few photographs of active churches. When planning a work of this scope, it becomes difficult to determine without causing offense when an individual or church should be included, or when one should be omitted. The copy negatives and their prints form a photo archive that we hope will become a treasured resource to help future generations understand how Stark County then became Stark County now.

BIBLIOGRAPHY

Atlas of Stark County, Ohio (New York: F.W. Beers and Company, 1870).

Basner, Ruth Harpold, *Yesteryears* (Virginia Beach, Virginia, 1996).

Blue, Herbert Tenney Orren, *History of Stark County, Ohio: From the Age of Prehistoric Man to the Present Day,* 3 vols. (Chicago: S. J. Clarke Publishing Company, 1928).

Canton Repository, *100 Years of Stark County Remembered* (Canton: *The Canton Repository,* 1999).

Danner, John, *Old Landmarks of Canton and Stark County, Ohio* (Logansport, Indiana: B. F. Bowen, 1904).

Hayden, Sarah Ross and Dunham, Jim, *Coming Home to Canton* (Montgomery, Alabama: Community Communications, Inc., 2002).

Heald, Edward Thornton, *A Brief History of Stark County: A digest of Mr. Heald's six-volume Stark County Story,* 1st ed. (Canton: The Stark County Historical Society, 1963).

Heald, Edward Thornton, *The Stark County Story*, 9 vols. (Canton: Stark County Historical Society, 1949-1959).

Kauffman, William J., *Atlas of Stark County, Ohio* (Canton: The Ohio Map and Atlas Company, 1896).

Kuhns, William T., *Memories of Old Canton and My Personal Recollections of William McKinley* (Canton: Privately published, 1937).

Lehman, John H., *A Standard History of Stark County*, 3 vols. (Chicago: The Lewis Publishing Company, 1916?)

New Historical Atlas of Stark County, Ohio (Philadelphia: L. H. Everts and Company, 1875).

Perrin, William Henry, ed., *History of Stark County, with an Outline Sketch of Ohio* (Chicago: Barkin & Baltey, 1881).

Roseboom, Eugene Holloway, and Weisenburger, Francis P., *A History of Ohio* (Columbus: Ohio Historical Society, 1973).

LISTING OF STARK COUNTY SITES ON THE NATIONAL REGISTER OF HISTORICAL PLACES

http://www.nationalregisterofhistoricplaces.com/OH/Stark/state.html

Bethlehem Twp.
Loew-Define Grocery Store and Home, 202 S. Market St., Navarre
Stahl-Hoagland House (Edwards House), 330 W. Wooster St., Navarre

Butler Twp. (Alliance)
Alliance Bank Building (Bank One), 502 E. Main St., Alliance
Eagles Building – Strand Theater (Wallace Building), 243 E. Main St., Alliance
Earley-Hartzell House (Mabel Hartzell Museum), 840 N. Park Ave., Alliance
First Methodist Episcopal Church (Christ United Methodist Church), 470 E. Broadway, Alliance
Glamorgan Castle, 1025 S. Union Ave., Alliance
Haines House, 186 W. Market St., Alliance
Maudru House (private dwelling), Alliance
Mount Union College District, Hartshorn St., Miller and Aultman Aves., Alliance

Constitution Twp. (Louisville)
St. Louis Church, 300 N. Chapel St., Louisville

Jackson Twp.
William Kettering Homestead, 5509 Wales Ave., Massillon

Lake Twp.
Hartville Hotel (Pantry Restaurant), 101 N. Prospect St., Hartville
Lake Township School (Board of Education), 1101 Lake Center St., Uniontown
John Miller House (Lewis Miller House), 9677 Cleveland Ave., NW, Greentown
Harry Bartlett Stewart Property, 13340 Congress Lake Rd., Hartville

Lawrence Twp.
Canal Fulton Historic District (Ohio-Erie Canal, Market, Canal, Cherry, and High Streets), Canal Fulton

Lexington Twp.
Science Hill School, 11810 Beeson St., Alliance

Marlboro Twp.
New Baltimore Inn, 14722 Ravenna Ave., NE, New Baltimore

Massillon Twp. (Massillon)
First Methodist Episcopal Church (First United Methodist Church), 301 Lincoln Way East, Massillon

First National Bank Building (Lincoln Professional Building) 11 Lincoln Way West, Massillon

Five Oaks (Massillon Women's Club, J. Walter McClymond's Residence), 210 4th St. NE, Massillon

Fourth Street Historical District (roughly bounded by 3rd, 5th, and Cherry Streets and Federal Ave.), Massillon

Ideal Department Store Building (Snyder-Hess Building), 55-59 Lincoln Way East, Massillon

Massillon Cemetery Building, 1827 Erie St. S., Massillon

Spring Hill, Wales Rd., NE, Massillon

St. Mary's Catholic Church (Catholic Church of St. Mary, Mother of God), 206 Cherry Rd., NE, Massillon

St. Timothy's Protestant Episcopal Church, 226 3rd St. SE, Massillon.

McKinley Twp. (Canton)
Barber-Whitticar House, 519 Cleveland Ave., SW, Canton

Bender's Restaurant (Belmont Buffet), 137 Court Ave. SW, Canton

Canton Public Library, 236 3rd St. SW, Canton

Case Mansion, 1717 N. Market Ave., Canton

City National Bank Building, 205 Market Ave. S., Canton

George E. Cook House (Vadose Research Center, Corman Health Care), 1435 Market Ave. N., Canton

Dewalt Building, 122 Market Ave. N., Canton

Eagles' Temple, 601 S. Market Ave., Canton

Harry E. Fife House (Beck Home), 606 McKinley Ave., SW, Canton

First Ladies' National Historic Site: 205 Market Ave. S. and (Saxton House) 331 Market Ave. S., Canton

First Methodist Episcopal Church (Church of the Savior United Methodist Church), 120 Cleveland Ave. SW, Canton

First Lutheran Church, 909 E. Tuscarawas St., Canton

First Reformed Church (First United Church of Christ), 901 E. Tuscarawas St., Canton

Frances Apartment Building, 534 Cleveland Ave., SW, Canton

Garnet B. French House, 2410 Cleveland Ave., Canton

Harvard Company – Weber Dental Manufacturing Company (Factory Industrial Supply), 2206 13th St. NE, Canton

Hotel Courtland (St. Francis Hotel, Stark County Office Building), 209 W. Tuscarawas St., Canton

Landmark Tavern, 501 E. Tuscarawas St., Canton

Brooke and Anna E. Martin House (Shurman-Martin House), 1627 Market Ave. N., Canton

William McKinley Tomb, 7th St. NW, Canton

Mellett-Canton Daily News Building, 401 W. Tuscarawas St., Canton

Old McKinley High School, 800 N. Market Ave., Canton

Onesto Hotel, 2nd St. and Cleveland Ave., NW, Canton

Palace Theater, 605 Market Ave., N., Canton

Harry S. Renkert House (Amateur Hall of Fame, Belden House), 1414 Market Ave., N., Canton

Ridgewood Historical District, bounded by Gibbs Ave., NE, Frazer Ave., NW, 25th St. and 19th St., Canton

August Schuffenecker Building, 134 6th St. SW, Canton

St. John's Catholic Church, 6th St. and McKinley Ave., NW, Canton

St. Peter Church, 720 Cleveland Ave., NW, Canton

Stark County Courthouse and Annex, Market Ave., N., and Tuscarawas St., W., Canton

Third Street Bridge, 3rd St. SE., Canton

Henry H. Timken Estate Barn, 13th St. NW and I-77, Canton

Trinity Lutheran Church, 415 W. Tuscarawas St., Canton

Vicary House, 3730 Market Ave., N., Canton

Osnaburg Twp.
Clearview Golf Club, 8410 Lincoln St. SE, East Canton

Werner Inn (Reed Tavern, Kendzora House), 131 E. Nassau St., East Canton

Perry Twp.
Bordner House (Jack A. Cady House), 4522 7th St. SW, Canton

Plain Twp.
Jacob H. Bair House (Charles D. Homer House), 7225 N. Market Ave., North Canton

Hoover Farm, Easton St., North Canton

Sandy Twp.
Elson-Magnolia Flour Mill, 261 N. Main St., Magnolia

Seven Ranges Terminus (monument), west of Magnolia at junction of the Stark, Tuscarawas, and Carroll County lines.

Sugar Creek Twp.
Brewster Railroad YMCA/Wandle House, 45 S. Wabash Ave., Brewster

Walter S. Putman House (Stotzer House), 303 Lawnford Ave., Wilmot

Emanuel and Frederick Serquet Farm, Wilmot

Wilmot United Brethren Church, Massillon St., Wilmot.

Public Survey in Stark County

Years noted are the 1st survey dates.
Some townships have 2 dates due to
that land being the boundry between
the Indian territory and Settlers.

Lake Township 1800

Marlboro Township 1801

Lexington Township
1799

Lawrence Township
1800

1807

Jackson Township 1800

Plain Township 1801

Nimishillen Township
1800

Washington Township
1804

Tuscarawas Township
1800

Perry Township 1800

1807

Canton Township 1800

Osnaburg Township 1801

Paris Township 1803

Sugar Creek Township
1801

Bethelhem Township
1800

1807

Pike Township 1806

Sandy Township
1803

15

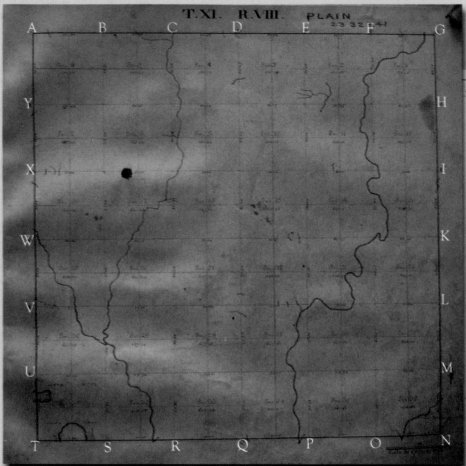

Illustrated is the map drawn from the 1801 Public Survey.
Note that letters around the map are identified by the type and size
of trees at the location. "A" has two trees, Elm 10 inches in diameter
and a Beech 7 inches in diameter.

MCKINLEY TOWNSHIP (CANTON)

Canton was established in 1805 by Bezaleel Wells. It was the first town to be settled in the area which later became Stark County. Learning of plans to split off a new county from Columbiana County, he acquired a site for a county seat centrally located in the new area. With this growth in mind he proceeded to build a roadway to connect Steubenville with New Lisbon. The Canton-Lisbon Road, known as State Road, became very important to the through traveler.

Two thoughts have surfaced as to reason the name of Canton was chosen. First is that he chose the name of the former estate near Baltimore, Maryland. Canton Estate owned by Captain J. O'Donnell who made his fortune trading with Canton, China. Another possibility may have been the Huguenot Family which raised Bezaleel. For the Huguenots, "Canton" means a geographical subdivision.

An original town plat was laid out on a treeless plain between two branches of the Nimishillen Creek. It had wide streets and a large public square, which is now Canton's central business district. By 1810 Canton had grown to 40 persons, they either operated or were served by a "grist mill, saw mill, general store, butcher shop, four taverns, a tannery, tailor shop, shoemaker, carpenter, wheelwright, doctor, lawyer, and school teacher". By 1820 Canton had a population of 504. Cleveland at the same time had 606.

The Pennsylvania and Ohio Railroad had been extended through Canton by 1852, causing a significant growth period. The C. Aultman Company, manufacturer of farm equipment relocated from Greentown to be near the railroad.

From 1851 to 1865 City Council had made 34 additions or 840 lots. The arrival of the Dueber-Hampden Watch Company in 1888, gave great growth to the city.

The area became known worldwide for being the the location of large industries, the largest watch factory in the world and the largest producer of farm equipment.

Then in 1896 Canton again became the place to be with the election of its own William McKinley as President. With his famous Front Porch Campaign, he drew many thousands to the area.

William McKinley, 25th President of the United States

William McKinley and parents

William McKinley Sr.   Nancy Allison McKinley

Nancy Saxton McKinley and parents

James A. Saxton   Katherine DeWalt Saxton

Birth place in Niles, Ohio.*

On the farm in Minerva , Ohio.

DR RIXEY. FARMER "JACK" ADAMS. COLONEL MYRON T. HERRICK.
PARMALEE HERRICK. PRESIDENT McKINLEY. SECRETARY CORTELYOU.

As a young soldier.*

Entering First Methodist Church in Canton, Ohio.

Home on 8th and Market, N., Canton, Ohio.

Parade during the 1896 Campaign for President.*

McKinley giving speech on his front porch on Ladies Day.*

A crowd came to hear McKinley give speech from the front porch of his home.*

Dining with Senator Hanna and other dignitaries.

William and Ida relaxing in their study.

Prior to speech in Buffalo.

During his first speech in Buffalo.

With Vice President Theodore Roosevelt.*

20

Carriage with casket approching the Stark County Court House.

Honor Guard, escorting the slain President.*

Placing the casket in the Court House for public viewing.*

President Theodore Roosevelt arriving to view the President.

Arch erected in honor of McKinley by the Canton Public Schools.

First tomb for President McKinley at the West Lawn Cementry.*

First Methodist Church arrangement for the funeral.*

Canton in mourning for the President.

McKinley National Memorial Trustees, Selecting Site For Monument.

From Left to Right- Cornelius N. Bliss, Wm. A, Lynch, Henry C. Payne, Alexander H. Revell, Myron T. Herrick, Marcus A. Hanna, Wm. McConway, John G. Milburn, Wm.R. Day, Charles W. Fairbanks, Fred S. Hartzell, George B. Cortelyou. *

Ground breaking for McKinley National Memorial.*

Early grading and construction.

Winter sets in and slows construction.

* Photos used by permission of the William McKinley Presidential Library and Museum, Canton, Ohio.

The McKinley Memorial with reflecting pool.

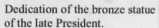

Dedication of the bronze statue of the late President.

Final resting place for William and Ida McKinley.*

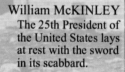

William McKINLEY
The 25th President of the United States lays at rest with the sword in its scabbard.

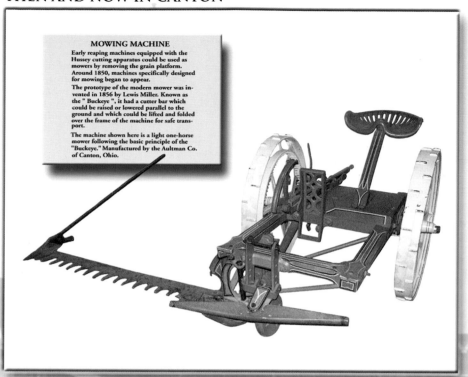

MOWING MACHINE

Early reaping machines equipped with the Hussey cutting apparatus could be used as mowers by removing the grain platform. Around 1850, machines specifically designed for mowing began to appear.

The prototype of the modern mower was invented in 1856 by Lewis Miller. Known as the "Buckeye", it had a cutter bar which could be raised or lowered parallel to the ground and which could be lifted and folded over the frame of the machine for safe transport.

The machine shown here is a light one-horse mower following the basic principle of the "Buckeye." Manufactured by the Aultman Co. of Canton, Ohio.

The Avalon Resturant of the 1950s is now a parking lot for Nationwide.

Canton City Auditorium was between 4th and 5th Streets on Cleveland Ave.

Barnett Hotel, East Tuscarawas and Cherry in the 1920s. Now SARTA connector terminal.

Canton Post Office 1894, now the Frank T. Bow Federal Building.

West Tuscarawas St. between Court and Cleveland Ave., when it was filled with small businesses. Now the block has parking and an ice rink.

6th and Market Ave. South, Eagles Building, on the site of the home of Frank S. Lahm, friend of the Wright Brothers and Canton aviation pioneer William H. Martin.

Canton Grocery and Warehouse, which later became Dannenmiller Grocery Warehouse.

Canton Christian Home, 2600 N. Cleveland Ave. formerly Stark County Home for the Aged.

Present First Christian Church on land of Stark County Home on North Cleveland Ave.

Fowell Building in the early 1900's, It has gone through many face lifts.

The Grand Opera House was on Piedmont and 3rd S.E. Now the side of the Marriott-McKinley Hotel.

Aerial view looking northwest going up Cleveland Ave.

Jacob Lehman Furniture Manufacturing, South Market Ave. 1940's

First Trust Savings and Loan later became Unizan Bank.

N. Market at 6th Street. Hotel Belden was demolished, The property is now a vacant lot.

County Home on Cleveland Ave. NW, now Main Post Office.

Looking East on Tuscarawas St. from Public Square 1900's.

From the air looking southeast over Little Italy, Now Timken and Detroit Diesel.

Ohio Power Office Building at 2nd and Cleveland SW, in the 1920s.
Now American Electric Power.

Orrin McIntire's Photo Studio, east side of the square 1850s, now County Office Building.

Pro Football Hall of Fame, 1962 and now.

Zebulon Davis Home between 13th and 14th Streets on N. Market St.

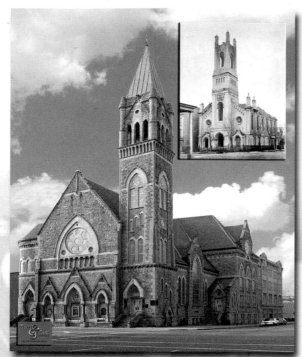

First Methodist Episcopal Church, 1881, now Church of the Savior United Methodist church home of William McKinley.

Case Mansion at 17th and Market N., formerly Canton Art Institute.

Canton Water Works Park with Canton Electric Generation Plant 1920's.

C. Aultman's Double Star Steam Tractor and today's equipment to do the harvest.

Stark County Courthouse thru different stages of construction and renovation from 1816 to 2005.

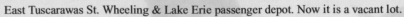

East Tuscarawas St. Wheeling & Lake Erie passenger depot. Now it is a vacant lot.

Looking north on Market St. from 4th St. South in the early 1900's.

Fawcett Stadium 1949, McKinley-Massillon Game. Today, the Pro Football Hall of Fame.

The G.A.R. Band, looking northeast from 3rd St. with the Unizan Bank.

Seitner's Department Store. 3rd and Market St. South, today it is a parking deck.

12th St. NW, looking west from Market Ave.

George D. Harter Estate, now Canton Civic Center.

Dueber-Hampden Watch Works placed above it's original location. Demolished early 1960's. for the construction of I-77.

The McKinley Hotel in the early 1900s. Row of Model "T" Fords being delivered to Baskerville Motors on the west side of street.

East Tuscarawas St. looking west from the Wheeling & Lake Erie tracks.

Looking north on Market St. from Central Plaza.

Looking north on Market St. with the St. Edward's restoration. A 1905 Cadillac is pulling 8 tons of steel.

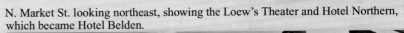

N. Market St. looking northeast, showing the Loew's Theater and Hotel Northern, which became Hotel Belden.

3rd and McKinley SW in the 1920s, when gas was cheaper. Now U.S.A. Quickprint.

The McCrory building built by the *Canton Repository*, now a Rite-Aid.

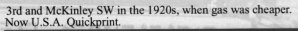

Southeast corner of Public Square 1900s, now the County Office Building.

Then Stark County Jail, now the Stark County Water and Animal Control Departments.

The Saxton Home, then the Key Shop and a furniture store. Now National First Ladies Library.

C. Aultman & Co., which manufactured Farm equipment from the 1850s, now vacant and Hercules Motors.

The Savings and Loan Co., now county offices at W. Tusc and Court Ave.

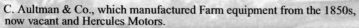

First National Bank in the early 1900s. The current building was built in 1923. Now Bank One.

Downtown Ford, yesterday and today.

Ewing Chevrolet, Cleveland Ave. NW, in the 1940s and as it looks today.

Ohio Theater at 4th and Market Ave. N. Now a parking lot.

St. Peter's Church and Rectory in the early 1920s, now the church and school.

Bill Simpson Cigar Store was a spot for fun as you can see this cow in the street, plus they made the best milk shakes in town.

We have come a long way from the one room school.

Stern & Mann served its early customers with personalized delivery shown here on South Market St. in the 1890s.

Schneider displays his materials by horse and wagon in the early days. Now there is a permanent showroom.

Late 1800s looking from the McKinley Hotel onto Public Square. Today's view is of Central Plaza as taken from the Unizan Bank Building.

Looking north on Central Plaza in the early 1900s with a circus was coming to town, And the view today.

Courtland Hotel later became the St. Francis, and is now the ice rink and a spot for lunch.

1914 Canton Jitney Bus 5 cents a ride downtown Then and Now.

Looking northwest from 3rd and Market South in the late 1800s. People are watching a parade during McKinley's front porch campaign.

Looking northeast on central plaza with Citizens Savings and Harter Bank.

Kempthorn Motors of the 1950's. And as it appears today.

BETHLEHEM TOWNSHIP

Prior to 1815, Bethlehem and Pike Townships were included in Canton Township. A portion of Tuscarawas Township, organized in 1810, also went into the new township, created in March of 1815 and named for the Pennsylvania hometown of the German and English settlers who had migrated to the area.

By the time that Bethlehem Township held a seperate election in 1817, the community of Bethlehem (later to become Navarre) had a log school house and a log church; and the days of Indians crossing the Muskingham Trail and of Christian Frederick Post's mission work were fading in the minds of pioneers looking for fertile land and rich resources.

The township was heavily timbered and, with the exception of the village of Navarre, has maintained its rural character.

Nickles Bakery transportation 1909 and today.

Nickles Bakery circa 1950 and today

Oven for baked goods 1909 and today's automated lines.

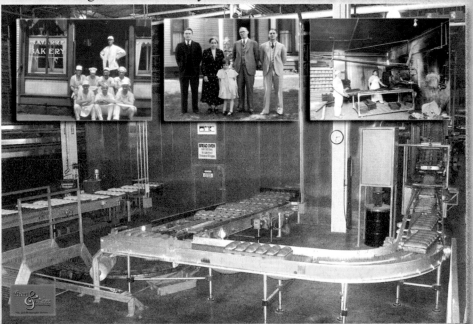

Expansion of Nickles Bakery over the lock on the Ohio-Erie Canal

Location where William McKinley tried his first lawsuit. Owned today by Altercare.

Enos Raffensberger Home, owner of a lumber yard, circa 1840, Owned today by Harry Stebbins

Original genealogy of Joseph Mathews family. Home built 1836. Now home of the Navarre-Bethlehem Twp. Historical Society.

Navarre Village Hall circa 1890s and new building constructed in the 1950s

Balough Avenue looking north over the Tuscarawas River and the Ohio-Erie Canal

Southwest Corner of Rochester Square showing the grain warehouse in the 1890s, now home for small businesses and apartments

Ernest Nickles Home yesterday and today, now owned by Joel Dutton.

Center Square looking west 1890s and today

Village of Navarre Fire Dept., then and now.

Navarre House Hotel, Center Square, circa 1900s. Today it is a flea market.

Bird's eye view of the Navarre Flood of 1913 and the same area today.

44

Feedmill circa 1900s, today Surbey Feed and Supply.

Navarre Union School late 1800's. Today it is an elementary school.

Navarre Post Office 1900. Today the site has apartments and vacant buildings.

Service station on Bethelhem Square, now a residence.

Main Street looking north over the Wheeling & Lake Erie Railroad, then and now.

Rochester House on Rochester Square, today a business and residence

Rhine Home late 1890s, famous for baking large pretzels and peddling them door to door.

Looking northeast on Center Street from Rochester Square, late 1890s and today

BUTLER TOWNSHIP (ALLIANCE)

An early leader, Matthias Hester, recorded that in September 1850, the village was first known as Liberty. Soon thereafter another founding father Elisha Teeters purchased 80 acres along the Ohio and Pennsylvania railroad from Union Ave. to Liberty Ave. There was a public sale of the lots in 1851 and the population recorded was 250. In this manner the village grew-spurred on by the prosperity of the railroads, factories, businesses and the surrounding productive farms. Because of this prosperity, the citizens petitioned to change the name of Liberty to Alliance in 1854.

By 1860 Alliance boasted more than 500 lots and extened from Union Ave. to Webb Ave. and from Vine to Oxford Streets with a population of 1300. Gathering momentum, Mount Union was absorbed into Alliance in 1888 and by 1900 there were more than 9000 residents living and working here.

1910 Glamorgan Castle, with today's Castle.

Looking west on Main St. circa 1900, and as it looks today.

Northeast corner of State St. and Union Ave. with the College Inn, circa 1940 and today.

Union and State Streets looking north, circa 1908, and the same view today.

Railroad Station 1901, with McKinley's funeral train on its way to Canton.

The Judd House circa 1885, now the Adminstration Building for Mt. Union Collage.

Public Square 1890, now known as Freedom Square.

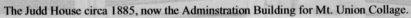

City Hospital in 1901, now Alliance Community Hospital

Alliance City Central Fire Station in 1907, now home of the Carnation City Players.

Carnegie Free Library circa 1940, now senior apartments.

Alliance High School built in 1910, now Towers Apartment for senior citizens.

Opera House collapse in 1886, then and now an empty lot.

Alliance Country Club 1904, and circa 1940s with the current view.

The Chase House in 1900, now the intersection of Liberty and Main Streets.

American Steel Foundry in 1900, today Alliance Casting.

White Hollow early 1940s, today Hoover-Price Campus Center.

Sawburg Road overpass was a one lane bridge circa 1910. Now it is a two lane highway over the railroad tracks.

Conn House, on the southeast corner of Union and State Streets in 1836, and now the home of Walgreen's Drug Store.

Stanley Pool circa 1930s, today an empty lot.

1890s view of the southwest corner of Arch and Main Streets, with same view today.

Mt. Union Methodist Church in 1846, then and now. It is located at Union and Hartshorn Streets.

Looking South on Union Ave at State St.1908, Then & Now.

Meyers Home circa 1930. Now it is a Family Dollar store.

R.S. Kaylor Restaurant and Residence at 64 East Main St. in 1889, then and now.

CANTON TOWNSHIP

One of the five original townships created in March of 1809, Canton Township is the site of the largest city in Stark County and the county seat of government. The first settlers in the township were former land office entrepreneurs from Jefferson County, James F. Leonard and James and Henry Barber. They surveyed and platted Canton in 1805.

Communities in the township include Meyers Lake, North Industry and Waco.

North Industry was named to separate the community of East Sparta, since both had thriving industries at the time. The Congress Furnace Co. produced pig iron here in the early years. The coming of the Valley Railroad in the 1870's resulted in the opening of coal mines in the area. Workers drawn to the community by the mining operations, a flour mill, and lumber mill, built shanties, leading to the nickname "Slabtown." Lehmiller Hardware opened for business in 1881 by Jacob Lehmiller. North Industry was platted in 1891.

Waco originally was the site of several large farms. The county's first distillery, opened by John Sherrick on his farm in 1814, became Waco's first industry. When H.S. Belden found coal, clay and shale deposits on his farm in the 1870's, he started manufacturing paving bricks. His first contract was to pave the block in front of the Barnett Hotel on Cherry Ave., between Tuscarawas St. and Second St. SE. In the 1880's, the Canton Stoneware Company was built on the Sherrick farm. Waco continues to be primarly an industrial area.

Meyers Lake Park, in a photo taken in 1950; which now consists of condominiums on the lake front.

Hannon Electric Company founded in 1926 grew to the present building in 1985.

Lehmiller Hardware, a busy supply house in the early 1920s, is now a vacant building.

The Meyers Lake Rocket Ride out over the lake was anchored to the center pole located where the gazebo is now.

Canton Township Transit Company operated the school buses in the 1930s. Now they are operated by the Canton Local School District.

Those visiting the park could ride on a boat around the lake shore. Now it harbors boats for those who live there.

The lake had a shallow area that made a pleasant beach for all to swim. It has been modified to dock the many boats.

American Legion in a parade in the 1930's, going north on Ridge Avenue.

Moonlight Ballroom in the days of the Big Bands. It is now hidden by houses and trees.

Canton South High School, then and now. The growth is not evident here but does show behind the current building.

Peace Evangelical Lutheran Church in 1876, now the Canton Local School District Board of Education.

Meyers Lake Roller Coaster provided many thrilling rides. The end of it is marked by this large boulder.

The Samuel Yoder home, located on Ridge Ave., in 1916 and today with a few home modifications.

A bridge was constructed over the lake for those who did not want to swim across.

The beach house on Meyers Lake is now boat docks.

Finney's Drug Store in the early Southgate Shopping Center, has been changed to One Pharmacy.

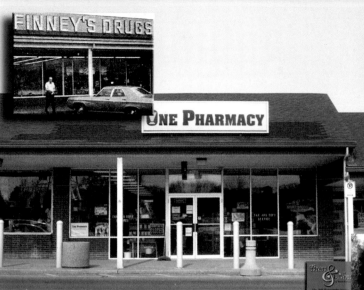

Ridge Ave. was a main street having many shops, such as Charles Henry's meats, boots and shoes.

The picnic pavillion at Meyers Lake was a spot to get out of the hot sun and get a refreshing drink. It is now covered by undergrowth.

The Old Landmark Tavern on Ridge Ave has retained most of its old appearance.

The Old Landmark Tavern had many antiques on its walls, which have been replaced by advertising.

Meyers Lake Park

JACKSON TOWNSHIP

Jackson Township was organized in 1815 as part of Plain Township. Jackson Township was named in honor of General Andrew Jackson who became the seventh President of the United States. McDonaldsville, the first village to be platted and recorded in Jackson Township, was its only permanent community for the first 100 years. The village was recorded in 1829 and is said to be named for an officer McDonald, who served under General Marion in the Revolutionary War.

Two of the county's cleanest streams flow in opposite directions through the township: one heads northwest into Willowdale; the other south through Lake O' Springs, Lake Cable, and Sippo Creek. Both streams empty into the Tuscarawas River at different points. Early settlers found the Mudbrook and Millbrook creeks advantageous for operating mills. Daniel Slanker built the first sawmill in 1820. The grist and flour mill, established by Slanker and Michael Sprankel, later became the brewery of the Massillon Brewing Company. When this building burned in 1905, the foundation stones were used to erect a new mill in 1925.

Early settlers in this area were of German descent, mostly coming from Pennsylvania. Slanker laid out Millport in 1835 along the canal. The settlement was vacated 13 years later. The post office there was named Crystal Springs; the railroad stop was known as Milburn. Both are gone today, as well.

Two churches established early in the township are St. Jacob's Lutheran on Mudbrook Rd, established in 1815, and the EUB church at Mc Donaldsville, formed in 1835.

The only incorporated village in this township is Hills and Dales, which has its own unique history and position in the county.

Sunset Hills Burial Park, established by Richard T. Smart in 1954, is located on Everhard Rd. NW in Jackson Township. East of the cemetery, once swampland and share crop property, ground was broken in 1969 for Belden Village. The name was changed to Westfield Shoppingtown in 2003.

Jackson Center School, established in the mid 1800's was moved and restored by the Jackson Township Historical Society in 2000. Relocated on Fulton Road NW in Jackson Township opened it to the public Oct. 2002.

Jackson Sauder Middle School was the former Jackson Township Consolidated School in 1930. Located on Mudbrook St. northwest Jackson Township.

This 1832 sandstone residence was once the home of Thomas and Francis Kirkpatrick from England. He discovered coal deposits on his land and in 1833 opened the first coal mine in Stark County. It is located on Jane Street NW.

Jackson Township local school buses.

Jackson Center School interior. Pupil insert shows the First thru the Eighth grade with Mr. Preston Lawrence, teacher in 1952.

Smith Mill was established in 1952 by Richard W. Smith and his son Walter. It was commonly known as a mill where apples were pressed for cider. The water-fed turbine which once operated the machinery has been restored. Located in Crystal Springs on Erie Ave. NW.

Ground was broken for Brunnerdale Seminary in 1930 for a monastery to house members of the Society of the Most Precious Blood, and a high school for boys wanting to enter the priesthood. The property was sold in 1989 and developed into homes, condos, and a private golf course, now the Glenmoor Country Club. Located on Brunnerdale and Hills and Dales Roads.

The John H. Carnes farm had coal removed from the property by the Betty Coal Co. in 1928. The farm was located on Pinelane Street in northwest Jackson Township.

Boulder Marker commemorates a 1785 treaty between the Wyandot, Delaware, Chippewa, and Ottawa Indians and the United States, whereby the river became part of the boundary line between theUnited States and the territory of the Indians. Located on Erie Ave, in northwest Jackson Township.

Once known as "Farmers Delight," the former homestead was built by Henry Bachtel in 1832. The nine-room southern style was built of brick manufactured from clay taken from the estate's fields. Located on Portage Road NW, the developed farmland is known as "The Meadowlands."

Mc Donaldsville St. Paul's United Methodist Church was built in 1829. After 5 major experiences in church building, the present church was erected in McDonaldsville on Wales Rd. NW.

The first half of Lake Cable Shopping Center was constructed in 1945. The second half was completed in 1951. It was the first of its kind in the township. It is located on Fulton Road NW.

Built in 1899 by Hiram S. Clay. The barn housed dairy cows. The Joseph Tilton family resided here in 1940 to 1960. Sunny Brook Farm is located on Fulton Road.

Once pasture land and streams, William C. Hensel purchased this land and founded Rose Lane Health Center in 1962.

Jackson Township Safety-Service Building was dedicated June 8, 2003, and houses the police and fire department along with administrative offices. It is located on the former Kettering-Yearkey Farm on the corner of Wales Ave. and Fulton Road in northwest Jackson Township.

This house was built in 1884 by William and Susan Kettering. Kettering was a prominent wheat farmer in the area. Later, the Charles Yearkey family occupied the home. The house was relocated in 1988 to its present site on Fulton Rd. NW.

Harry Albrecht family owned 350 acres of farmland which was sold in1927 to make way for Tam O'Shanter golf course. The barn on Fulton Road NW became the maintenance barn for the golf course.

1968

1902

1834

St. Jacob's Church, also known as Mudbrook Church, evolved from 1815 log cabin. In 1834, a brick building was erected with separate entrances for men and women. It was replaced by a frame building in 1902. A new building dedicated in 1968 rests on some of the original foundation. Located on Mudbrook Road NW.

Noble's Pond development was farmland once owned by the Noble sisters. In the 1920s Maurice Koehler leased the land to operate a flying field for small aircraft. The business closed in 1954. Located on Wales Rd. NW.

The remains of an early stage coach inn, dismantled in the 1930s, was located off Amherst Road where Audubon Ridge was developed.

Ground was purchased for Willowdale in 1918 by C. W. Stuart Realty Co. Spring rains in 1922 caused the earthen dam to be washed out. A concrete dam was built soon after.

In 1923 when Austin B. and Dueber S. Cable purchased their first tract of land needed to create Lake Cable, Fulton Road was a dirt road west of Everhard. In the summer of 1926, it was paved with fifteen-inch brick.

Built in the 1820's by Daniel Slanker, this was the highest structure in the township at the time. The grist mill was torn down in 1925. The original stone foundation remained. In 1928, Albert Rohr converted the grounds to the High Mill Swimming Park until it was sold in 1965. In 2002 a tornado did extensive damage leaving the park's future in question.

LAKE TOWNSHIP

On June 4, 1816, the Stark County Commissioners organized the 12th township of Lake. Originally a part of Plain Township, Lake Township is 33.5 square miles in area, which is about average size for the seventeen townships in Stark County. Lake Township has within its boundaries the incorporated village of Hartville, which in December 2001 had a land area of 2.5 square miles and a population of 2,174, making it the fourth most populated village in Stark County. Unincorporated villages include Cairo, Greentown, and Uniontown; the hamlets of Midway and Mt. Pleasant, and the historic village of Aultman.

From Lake Township Historical Society book *"Introducing Lake Township,"* Elmer S. Yoder, Editor.

Schumacher Lumber Company

Lake Center School was established in 1850 at the corner of Lake Center St. and King Church Rd. Property of Lake Township Historical Society.

Hartville Kitchen was established as Country Kitchen Restaurant in 1966. Hartville Market Place was established as the livestock auction in 1939.

Uniontown School was established in 1820. A new school was completed in 2001.

Greentown's Howard D. Miller American Legion Post #436

Greentown looking south in 1907 and 2004 (State St. and Cleveland Ave. NW)

Hartville High School, built in 1820 on High St.

Hartville Pie Factory was established as the Hartville Hotel at the corner of Prospect St. and Rt. 619.

Greentown Square (State and Cleveland Ave.,NW) looking northwest, in 1907 and 2004.

Tile and Conduit Works of Aultman, established in 1881. Made conduits for underground telephone lines.

Werstler Farm, established 1815, just north of Cairo.

Greentown looking west on State Street in 1907 and 2003.

Downtown Hartville on Flag Day, 1917.

Greentown looking east on State Street in 1907 and 2003.

Greentown, looking north on Cleveland Ave. from State Street, in 1907 and 2003.

Longaberger Basket Factory, established as the Asplin Basket Factory.

Hartville looking east on Rt. 619 and Rt. 43 in the 1920s and 2003.

Mourners waiting for McKinley's train at Hartville Railroad depot in 1901.

Hartville looking southeast on Rt. 619 and Rt. 43 in the 1920s and 2003.

Conrad Brumbaugh's log cabin　Mr. & Mrs Harry B. Stewart　Conrad Brumbaugh

1907

Quail Hollow State Park, formerly the Harry B. Stewart mansion

Peter Zepp, a blacksmith in Greentown, was established in 1907 at the corner of Schlemmer Pl. and Brown Ave. NW.

Looking southeast on Cleveland Ave from the square in Greentown.

The original clay works (1870) was located south of State St. at the railroad in Aultman.

Greentown 1907

1870 before Tile and Conduit Works

LAWRENCE TOWNSHIP

Originally part of Plain Township, Lawrence Township was separated in 1810 and platted in 1815. The township was named for Captain James Lawrence of the U.S. Navy who had become famous for his War of 1812 quote, "Don't give up the ship." This quotation later was adopted as the township's motto. The founders divided the area into 36 square-mile sections split diagonally by the Tuscarawas River.

Henry Clapper and Henry Lower first settled the area in 1809 and Col. William Goudy built the gristmill in 1812. However, there were no settlements east of the river before 1812. The early settlers came by canoe or by wagon along the state road. The township's first clerk, James Leonard, made history when his marriage to Sarah Barber, June 6,1806, was the first wedding to take place in Stark County. The first store was opened by Henry A. Stidger in 1827.

Sullivan House, built in 1879, is now the Canal Fulton Public Library.

Live and Let Live Saloon, circa 1900, which is now the Historic Canal Days Museum.

The G.A.R. in front of C.R. Daly Undertaking. It is now occupied by Sewing Specialties by Karen.

The Canal St. Union Block Building, looking south from Market St.

Canal Fulton School (1886), between Market and Cherry Sts. at Locust. Now a play ground for the elementary school.

1913 Flood on the east side of Fisher Tin Shop, and the same view today.

Front Hotel Bloomfield, circa 1915, and same location now.

North Canal Street circa 1900, with Finefrock Funiture Delivery wagon, and the same view today.

Liberty St. (Market St.) looking west from Market Square, and the same view as it appears today.

Market Street stone bridge, circa 1900, and as it looks today.

Smoke and fire marking the demise of the Opera House. The Canal St. Teddy Bear Shop now occupies the site.

Cherry St. turtle back bridge, early 1900s, which today is the entrance to Community Park.

Billings Dry Goods, circa 1880, which is now a laundromat.

The Oberlin House was built by Sarah and Christian Oberlin. The house has been restored.

1913 Flood watchers at the Hotel Bloomfield Market St., which is now the home of Coach House Florist.

Canal St. looking north in the 1920s and as it is today.

North Market St. after the 1904 flood, looking from across the canal and the same view today.

Installing telephone lines at Brimstone Corners in 1901, located at the intersection of Cherry St. (Rt. 93) and Canal St.

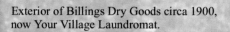

The City Hotel which stands where The Heritage Society Museum has its headquarters.

Exterior of Billings Dry Goods circa 1900, now Your Village Laundromat.

Schalmo & Son, showing the arrival of McCormick Deering tractors. This became the Post Office, then later, Toys Time Forgot.

Great Western Opera House prior to 1930, located at Brimstone corner, which is the current location of Stan Snopel Insurance.

The 1913 flood looking east across the Tuscarawas River from the canoe livery, showing damage to the Cherry St. Bridge.

View of flood from the roof of Finefrock Furn. Now the bridge over the canal has been removed. The site is the entrance to Community Park.

LEXINGTON TOWNSHIP

Lexington Township was named for the famous battle of the Revolutionary War. It is located in the northeast corner of Stark County bounded by Portage and Mahoning Counties. The first land owners were Quakers, who came to the area about 1805, locating just west of Route 225 north of Alliance. Lexington village had the first post office in the township. All that remains are a few homes and a small church.

The Science Hill School, located on the corner of McCallum and Beeson Street is typical of those in use from 1876 thru 1956, when a new consolidated Lexington Township School was built. The building has been restored to circa 1920 by its owners, the Science Hill Historical Society.

Lexington Elementary School, built in 1956, houses students from Lexington, Greenbower, Sawburg, Bolton, and Science Hill schools. It is located on Atwater Ave. ½ mile north of Rt.619.

The home of Carolyn and Art Miller, located on German Church Street. Art purchased a 12 acre farm in 1944 and started a tree farm 10 years later.

The current post office is housed in a single trailer placed on this lot by the United States Postal Service in 1977. This lot was previously occupied by the A.J. Beltz Co., dealer in general merchandise.

Marlington High School was built in the early 1960s and consolidated the townships of Lexington, Marlboro, and Washington. It was built on property previously owned by John Pierre Domino, and later by his daughter and son-in-law the George Oyster family.

Zurbrugg's Cider Mill, owned by Ferdinand Zurbrugg, was located on the southwest corner of Beeson and Sawburg Ave. His son, L.V. Zurbrugg, shown leaning on the wheel, became heir to the mill and moved it to the opposite corner.

The Ben Snode Farm is now Tannenhauf Golf Course. It was built by Snode's three children and is still operated by his grandchildren. The farmhouse built in 1840 is still in use.

This is a school "Hack" used in the early 1900's to transport students to a drop off point where a larger motorized bus would take them to school.

This is the second building in Limaville. It was purchased by Francis Fox and remodeled into a double home. The first brick school was torn down in 1902.

The Terra Cotta Works was located next to the railroad and Price Street. It made marbles, jugs, crocks, small statues, and large ornamental yard statues.

Early Limaville post offices were located in the home of the Postmaster. The black and white insert was the post office on the corner of Jefferson and Church Streets where this home stands.

The Brethren Church of Limaville was purchased and made into a two family dwelling about the turn of the last century. The roof line shows the marks from the vestibule and bell tower.

The Paine Home was built in 1840 by Rufus Paine, a minister in Limaville. Now owned by Joyce and Duane Austin, it is being maintained much as it was originally.

Union Grove School built in 1859, served until 1934, the students transferred to Bolton. The building reverted to the original owner, Stanley Miller, whose son Wade Miller made it into a home.

The Standard Bolt and Manufacturing Company was built in 1901. They manufactured bolts, nuts, rivets, small forgings, and other specialties of iron and steel. It gave the name of Bolton to the area which had been known as Slabtown and Clayshaft.

A creamery was located on the south side of Main Street in Limaville. The building was abanded in the 1930s and the remains removed. A new home is now located on the site.

This was the location of the railroad station for Limaville. It was expected to become a thriving town until a second railroad bypassed the village, and growth came to a halt.

A large sign still proclaims this to be Fox's Garage. The overhang and gas pumps have been replaced with large doors. The building to the left was a grocery store.

The J.G. Coats Home also known as Green Hill was a very elaborate house on the corner of Price and McCallum. It started as a log cabin, with additions until it became the impressive Green Hill. It was all destroyed by fire in 1920 and never rebuilt.

The farm home of the late Benton I. Hoover located north of Beeson Street on the east side of McCallum Avenue. Recent owners have remodeled and added to the original structure.

MARLBORO TOWNSHIP

The first known records started back in 1785, when the birth of Marlboro Township followed closely the establishment of a new western boundary between Indian territory and the land claimed by settlers. The first known map was drawn in 1840. An original of this map hangs in the Rodman Public Library of Alliance, which indicates the edge of the Cuyahoga watershed and the creeks of the other outlying watersheds.

The organization of Marlboro Township took place March 4, 1816. It originally formed part of Lexington Twp. which shares its history. In the year 1805, Abraham Wileman cut the first stick of lumber in the township. The land of this was well as other townships, was entered at two dollers per acre, payable in three installments at the land office in Steubenville. When the government reduced the price to $1.25 per acre, there was a clause in the act permitting all who had forfeited their land, by not paying the second and third installments, to re-enter other tracts, at the rate of $1.25 per acre, to the amount they had paid on their forfeited entries. News was slow to travel, and the early settlers were long ignorant of the new clause. Rascals were standing by ready to take advantage of those who were not aware of the new clause and they would buy the new lands for a few dollars. Fortunes had their origin in this sharp practice, and one real estate operator, who started in this way, died worth a million and a half dollars.

Square of Marlboro, southwest corner. Picture taken in the late 1800's of Wearstlers General Store, which today is Townhall Antiques.

Public Square of Marlboro, late 1800's. Mr. Boyle waters his cow at the pump in the middle of the town.

Southwest corner of State Rt. 44 and Pontius St., in New Baltimore. Was Kuhn's General store, and is now the New Baltimore Antique Center.

Keifer's Village Blacksmith Shop next to the New Baltimore Community Church on Pontius St. in 1914.

New Baltimore Community Church in 1915, on Pontius St. in New Baltimore.

New Baltimore School on State Rt. 44, showing the first school buses known as "Hacks ". The bell from the tower was donated to Marlington High, which is now the Victory Bell.

Marlington Village School, (aka Union School), built in 1888. Now the Assembly of God Church on Marlboro Ave.

Marlboro Square. looking west on State Rt. 619 in the early 1900s.

Swamp Rd. looking east in the 1950s when the markets were open to the public for fresh vegetables.

Marlboro Square, showing the Methodist Church built in 1832. It is now an empty building.

Marlboro's Hotel in the 1800s. Sanners's Place sat on the southeast corner of Rt. 619 and Beechlawn.

Northwest corner of Marlboro Square in 1920, which is now the Marlboro Body Shop.

Bunker Hill School was built in 1866, then rebuilt with brick in 1890. Burned in 1960, today it is Vaughan's Hides and Furs on Smith-Kramer St.

E.A. Stevens General Store before fire in 1919, in New Baltimore on the corner of St. Rt. 44, and Pontius St.

Buckeye Packing in 1950, before the many expansions to make it what is today.

First residence built on Marlboro Square in 1823, by Dr. William Pennock, currently for sale.

Built in 1850, this house was used on the Underground Railroad prior to the Civil War. It is designated as an Historical site.

Marlboro Band and Fire Brigade, circa 1905. Looking north on Marlboro Ave.

Kozy Corner restaurant circa 1920. Now Candles Restaurant, the latest of many owners Located at State Rt. 44 and Swamp Road.

An empty building was once the Stage Coach Inn, also known as the Dew Drop Inn, on the southeast corner of Pontius St. and St.Rt. 44.

Center School, built in 1872, is now a private residence.

Lot shown on the northwest corner of Marlboro Square before the Fire Department was built in 1940.

Looking east on State Rt. 619 from Marlboro Square. The general store on right burned in 1935.

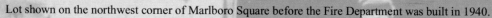

MASSILLON TOWNSHIP (MASSILLON)

Four separate villages merged to create the city of Massillon: Kendal, Massillon, West Massillon, and East Brookfield. Kendal was platted in 1812 by Thomas Rotch. James Duncan founded the second village, Massillon, in 1821. The third settlement was established in 1831 and used the name of West Massillon. The founder of this community was Judge William Henry who also co-founded Wooster. Henry also laid out the fourth village of East Brookfield in 1835.

Thomas Rotch visited Ohio and decided to settle in the Big Sippo Creek Valley. Rotch and his wife Charity brought with them a herd of 400 Merino sheep. He also built a woolen mill along the creek and a frame house on the land, which was called Spring Hill Farm.

James Duncan was a former sea captain from New Hampshire. In 1822, when the river reached flood stage he took a load of floor, bacon, potatoes and whiskey to Cincinnati. It was reported that he walked back because it was faster than coach travel.

The settlement on the east bank of the river was named by Mrs. Duncan for the Jean-Baptiste Massillon, a Roman Catholic French Bishop in the days of King Louis XIV.

From the collection of the Massillon Museum, gift of the Karl Spuhler Estate
The 1909 City Hall was razed in the mid 1970s for the new City Hall.

The James Duncan home, built around 1832, is now the Massillon Public Library.
From the collection of the Massillon Museum, gift of the Massillon Public Library

The Russell Home, circa 1890. It was razed in the mid 1960s. Now a Goodyear Store.
From the collection of the Massillon Museum

The Lincoln Theater opened in 1915. It thrived until 1977, when it became the Ten Star Theater until 1982. It then changed back to a movie house.

This building, built in 1850, has been remodeled and is used as an office building.

Lincoln Way looking west in 1847, with same view today.

First National Bank, built in 1920, Carvers Cigar Store back right, now Bank One.

South Side of Lincoln Way, looking west. This building was razed in the 1990s for Phase II of Massillon upgrading.

Massillon's YWCA and YMCA were formed in 1921. In 1973 the YMCA moved to Tremont St. The YWCA moved to the former United Way Building on 3rd Street.

The State Bank Company was founded in 1903. In 1938, it moved to the north side of Lincoln Way following the Depression.

OLJO Bowling Alley and the last blacksmith shop in Massillon, which were razed in 1966 to make way for a parking lot.

The north side of Lincoln Way West. The Arcade Market was razed to make way for Phase II upgrading in the 1980s.

The Merchants National Bank (1890-95) and later the Massillon Savings Banking Co. (1895-1912), renamed First Savings and Loan Company in 1912.

Oscar and William Bammerlin produced upright pianos in the early 1900s. The factory was on Factory Street, later moved to W. Main St., with a later plant on Mill St. The Main St. plant closed in 1933, the Mill St. location in 1975.

The Bee Hive was Massillon's main department store in 1883. A fire consumed the building along with others in November 1899.

This structure was built for Montgomery Ward, then occupied by A&P Grocery about 1931. Englehart Music occupied it until it was razed in 2002.

The Pennsylvania Railroad station was built 1870. The last Pennsylvania R.R. train stopped April 30, 1973, at which time Amtrak took over.

The Wellman Home in the mid 1800s, which is now the Red Carpet Inn.

Massillon's first Postmaster General, Mayhew Folger, was appointed in 1828. The Hess - Snyder Co. building was razed to make way for the current Post Office.

Lincoln Way Viaduct in the 1890s and today.

State Hospital Main Building around 1910, with the new buildings today.

Massillon City Hospital 1909, which is now Massillon Community Hospital.

West Tremont School, originally known as West Massillon Union School, was a $20,000 project when constructed in 1869.

NIMISHILLEN TOWNSHIP

Nimishillen Township, which surrounds the City of Louisville, was established in 1809. The name comes from the Nimishillen Creek, which flows through the area. One of the settlements in the township was in the northeast corner near what became the village of Harrisburg. A major attraction of the area was its timber, especially the abundant poplar and chestnut. Agriculture did not flourish here because of the clay content of the soil on higher ground and the large quantities of gravel in the low-lying areas.

Harrisburg was settled in 1827 by Pennsylvania Germans; Louisville in 1835. For a time, this was a stagecoach stop between Cleveland and Pittsburgh. When no railroad was constructed through the village, it became no more than a crossroads with businesses to serve only those residents from the immediate area.

Louisville, which outgrew Harrisburg, nearly had its beginnings as the village of Nimishillentown, which was platted by a group of Philadelphia land speculatores in 1807. The original plan to make Nimishillentown the Stark County seat never materialized.

Main Street, Louisville, looking northeast, then and now.

Northwest corner of Main and Mill Streets, Louisville.

St. Louis Hospice, on North Chapel Street.

95

Northeast corner of North Main and Mill Streets, once a blacksmith shop, and now the location of the SBC office.

Main St. looking southwest today, The Post office is shown with mail carriers and their mode of transportation

Louisville Public School in 1915, now the city's Safety Building

The Star Mill, then and now.

Paquelet Furniture as it appeared in 1900. Today it is an insurance agency.

Nist Geriatric Facility which became Greenmeadows Health Care Center.

Louisville Railroad Depot in 1900, now an empty lot.

Molly Stark Hospital in the early years, which is now a vacant building.

St. Joseph Hospice, now known as St. Joseph's Care Center.

The site of the Myers Home is today a playground for the St. Louis School.

Metzger's Hardware in the early 1900s, which today is a real estate office.

Looking southwest from railroad on West Main.

Looking south at vacant lot was Brahler Auto Body Shop, just west of the Eagles Building.

An Airstream trailer dealer sat on this corner looking west on Main and St. Louis Streets. Today a Dairy Queen is located there.

The Jones & Laughlin Steel Corp, which is now the Allegheny Ludlum Louisville Plant.

Louisville Motor Cars started here in the early 1900's. Many dealers have been at the same location, but today it is a vacant building.

Trolly turn-a-round at Depot St and W. Main, Then and Now

Peers Dairy Bar in the early 1900s, now drive-up bank teller.

Looking southeast on Main St. where the Post office was once located. The store was Schilling's in the early 1900s, and the Penny Alley today.

Louisville High School located on South Nickle Plate St.

Ron-L Restaurant sat at this location in the 1960's, Today, O.D. Miller is at same location.

Looking east on W. Main St. in the 1950s, where Yoder's Auto Service is today.

NORTH CANTON CITY

Prior to the 1800's, Indians roamed the forests that in the past two centuries have given way to the thriving community of North Canton. When Ohio became a state in 1803, pioneers from the east, primarily Pennsylvania Dutch, settled this Congress Lands area. Jacob Gaskins, a free slave, also bought land. His farmhouse was a stop on the Underground Railroad. The town of New Berlin was laid out by Samuel Bachtel in 1831. In reaction to World War I, citizens renamed the community North Canton in 1918. Hoover moved his tannery from his farm east of town in 1873. The Hoover Suction Sweeper was patented in 1908. The history of the town has been intertwined with that of the Hoover Company since the horse collar days. The town reached city status with the 1960 census and chose a charter form of government. Important elements in the growth of North Canton have been the early emphasis on education, religion, a strong work ethic, leisure time pursuits, and good transportation.

The North Canton square in 1961 (insert) and as it is today with Bitzer Park seen lower left.

Looking north on Main Street from the town square, auto traffic, the Hoover plant and City Hall have replaced the intcrurban, shown on its 1902 maiden voyage in the insert.

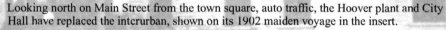

Erected in 2000, this lifelike bronze tribute to W. H. Hoover stands on the site of the New Berlin post office (left insert). Michael Bitzer's home in the right insert.

Grandparents graduated from North Canton High (left insert) from 1930 to 1957; moms and dads from Hoover High, south campus (right insert) until 1997; and now from the Hoover High north campus on Seventh St. NE.

A favorite spot, the Park movie theater (insert) is gone. The North Canton Public Library, built in 1953, and City Hall, built in 1971 are there now.

Parade units have marched past an ever changing block of buildings on South Main Street during the past century.

Photos at the intersection of Maple and Main Square show various businesses, including a grocery store, phone company operation and banking institutions.

A comparison of aerial views of downtown show growth -- wider streets, fewer residences, more commercial buildings.

The town center landmark, the Hoover Company, now Maytag, has occupied the north-east corner of the square since the tannery days (seen with the suction sweeper building about 1910).

The New Berlin School (insert) opened in 1888. A portion of the original grade school is part of the Portage School Building, now home to Montessori students.

Years ago the Mathie Dairy furnished milk to the townspeople from this site. The Memorial Stadium has been hosting football games and other events since 1947.

Cars stream south on N. Main St. along the same route where a century ago the interurban carried passengers from Canton to Akron.

Most people walked to work when the Hoover Office Building (insert) was moved across East Maple to serve as the Hoover Inn. The Inn has been replaced by an employee parking lot.

The Orchard Hill clubhouse, built on the former Gaskins farm in 1924, was destroyed by fire in 1986. The city has preserved the Arrowhead Country Club as The Fairways (now a dedicated Underground Railroad station site).

Since 1847 (left insert) St. Paul's Church has been growing and expanding to serve an ever-increasing number of area Catholic families.

The one constant in these two photographs looking south on Main Street, spanning about nine decades, is the St. Paul's Church steeple.

The family activity center, the Community Building YMCA on South Main, opened in 1970, replacing the Community Building given by "Boss" Hoover in 1923.

Religion plays a major role in North Canton. The 1872 Union Church (upper) was replaced in 1908 by (lower) a new building, renamed Community Christian in 1925 and dedicated in 1976.

Bill's Diner staff stood ready to serve their customers (insert), while today's City Hall offers a different kind of service from the North Main Street location.

These on the west side of S. Main St. date back to the 1920s with some changes and upgrades.

This playground north of the Middle School replaced the original Witwer Park in the 1960s, when the Lutherans relocated to the current Portage Street location.

The Zion Lutheran Church built on West Maple in New Berlin in 1905 (upper left) was enlarged (upper right) and then sold to the Presbyterian congregation in 1960, when the Lutherans relocated to the current Portage Street location.

North of town around Mount Pleasant Road, farm homes and interurban tracks have given way to a strip of commercial properties.

OSNABURG TOWNSHIP

Osnaburg, later to become East Canton, was a second village to be recorded in Stark County. It was laid out by James Leeper in the fall of 1806 and rivaled Canton until the latter was selected as the county seat in 1808.

The town was one of four military training spots in Stark County during the War of 1812. With seven hotels and the Reed and Wack Tavern, it became an important stopover before the advent of the railroad. By the time the railroad was built and the town was incorporated in 1880, only two hotels remained and there were just 507 residents in the community. Prior to 1896, coal mining was the leading industry in the area. John Merley organized the Canton and Osnaburg Brick Company in 1890. The firm was sold to the National Fireproofing Company of Waynesburg 10 years later, and the clay tile industry replaced mining as the leading industry of the area. Among those who played a prominent role in this industry was Enos Stewart, president of Stark Ceramics, who had a 23 year career as an educator before devoting himself exclusively to the manufacture of brick. Along with being known for the production of high grade ceramic products from the superior clays found in the region, East Canton is well known as an apple orchard center.

Werner Inn, or Reed Tavern, circa 1908.

East Canton Village Hall, little changed from years past.

Wack Tavern (Geib House), 1880s.

East Canton Fire Department, 1912 and today.

Stark Ceramics, Inc.

Osnaburg Railroad Station.

The Samuel W. Marks Farm, on Mapleton St. in 1885, now owned by the Varian family.

Bus Service, 1915 and today.

East Canton High School, with a group photo taken in 1926.

Mapleton United Methodist Church, originally the United Evangelical Church, founded in the early 1800s.

This residence was Mapleton School in the early 1900s.

Elisha Rice home on Lisbon St.

Centerville School, taught by Sadie Myers in the 1880's, is now a residence.

Evening Star School. Class photo was from around the 1890s.

Daniel Myers blacksmith shop, from around 1880, now the Church of God.

Schull Tavern, 1908 and today.

George Shoemaker Snyder farm on Mapleton St. which was a store and residence.

W. H. Snyder Hotel on Mapleton St.

Robert Cessna home.

William Werner built this building, now occupied by a flower shop.

The A.H. Flory Co. and Wallace Hardware occupied this building in the 1920s.

The DeHoff filling station, circa 1927 still serves the automotive public as East Canton Used Cars.

Nassau St. looking west.

PARIS TOWNSHIP

In 1818, a new township was formed from the eastern part of Osnaburg Township, It was given the same name as its first village which pre-dated the township by five years. In 1813 Rudolph Bair founded Paris. He chose this name because at that time Paris, France was considered the metropolis of the world. Two other small villages were formed in Paris Township, New Franklin about 1831 and Robertsville in 1842. Minerva, on the southeast corner of the township grew to be the largest village in the township.

The stagecoach traffic through New Franklin and Paris contributed to the growth of these communities and both were stops on the main east to west thoroughfare. These villages, as well as Robertsville and Minerva were well supplied with hotels, businesses, churches and schools. With the building of canals and the advent of the railroad, the small villages quickley lost out to other neighboring towns which were on the rail route.

Although there have been a lot of homes built in Paris Township over the years, it is still basically a rural community with a lot of acreage yet being farmed.

Looking north on Market St. from High St.in Minerva. Senior Order of Mechanics parade in 1911.

 The Minerva Post Office located on the property where, in 1919, Dr. McHenry bought the elaborate home built by John Shumaker. An earlier building at this same location was the Unger House, a hotel, 1844-1896.

Looking South on Market St. in Minerva, third building from the right was the Opera House. Market St. was originally named Mill St.

113

Cadillacs in front of the Commercial Hotel in New Franklin. The building is now a private home.

The orgin of the building on the northwest corner of the square in Paris is unknown, but for a long time in comparatively recent history, it was the Meiser Store where you could buy anything from groceries to notions to farm machinery.

Carl Dager's home beside the Grange Hall in Robertsville had to be moved to make way for the new Route 30.

Birdseye view looking northeast over Minerva from the W. Line St area.

The old Standard Oil station has been turned into a coffee shop and gift store. Located on the corner of Lincoln St. and Market St. in Minerva.

The earliest First Christian Church (then Disciples) in the town of Minerva was a brick structure which was located in the parking lot of the present building. The old one pictured here, built in 1888, burned in 1949 and the new one was built in three stages 1950, 1983 and 1993.

New Franklin square, looking east from just west of Rt.183 and Rt.172 crossroads with the Lutheran Church in the center.

The east side of Minerva's Market St. looking north from the High St. intersection.

The square in Paris. The Stagecoach Inn is on the left. The cannon has taken the place of the gazebo. The dark building on the right housed a general store and a barber shop.

The railroad station in Robertsville on Old Route 30.

The old mill in Paris that stood on the point where Paris and Beechwood Avenues formed a "Y".

This building, just south of the square in Paris, was used as a post office. For many years it was a meat market and is now a private home.

Until recently there was faded lettering on the back of this building on Valley St. in Minerva indicating that it was a Foundry. Since then it has been occupied by several different auto dealerships.

The second of two one room school houses in New Franklin. The first one burned and this one was dismantled and made into a shed on an area farm. The old buildings were immediately east of the still standing brick school, which was built in 1927.

Railroad station in Minerva.

Minerva High School, built in 1918. Now used as the middle school, it will soon be abandoned for the new middle school that is now completed. The first school was built in 1871.

This building on East Lincoln St. in Minerva was originally a car dealership.

Unger Hotel located on the northeast corner of High and Main St.

Roy Wickersham home located on the southwest corner of High and Main St.

Paris Railroad Station.

Little is known of this building, but was once the Kintner store and telephone office.

PERRY TOWNSHIP

Perry Township, formed by Stark County Commissioners on Dec. 7, 1813, was named in honor of Oliver Hazard Perry, hero of the War of 1812 victory near Put-in-Bay just three months earlier. The township, organized by Fred Stump, included portions of Lake and Tuscarawas townships. Its first community, Kendal, later became a part of Massillon. The first township election was held in February of 1814.

Perry, along with neighboring Jackson, Osnaburg, Sugarcreek and Tuscarawas townships, suffered a decline in population during the westward migration of the 1840-70s. Jonathan (Johnny Appleseed) Chapman is credited with planting the first orchard in Perry Township on the south side of the Canton/Massillon Road. The township is the site of the Massillon State Hospital, organized March 31, 1892. Site of the hospital, originally called the Eastern Ohio Asylum for the Insane, was chosen by William McKinley.

Mount St. Marie Academy- Central Catholic High School.

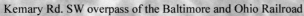

Kemary Rd. SW overpass of the Baltimore and Ohio Railroad

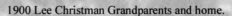

1900 Lee Christman Grandparents and home.

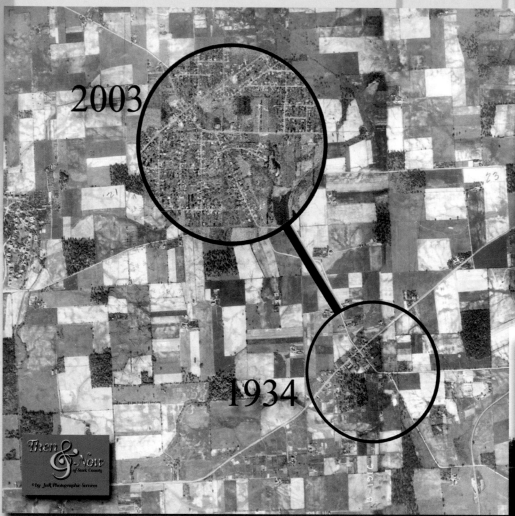

2003

1934

Aerial view of Navarre Rd. and Richville Drive. 1934 and 2003

Reedurban Elementary School, Perry Rd. S.W. looking north.

Intersection of Jackson Ave and Hankins St. 1970 and now.

Woodlawn Ave. looking south at 4th St. N.W.

Intersection of Genoa Rd. and 12th St. N.W.

Perry Dr. looking South at Lincoln Way.

Aerial of Lincoln Way East and Jackson Ave. 1934 and 2003.

2003

1934

Intersection of 12th St. N.W. and Woodlawn, looking south.

Perry Rd. looking South across railroad, with improved grade crossing.

Aerial of Lincoln Way and Woodlawn Ave. 1934 and 2003.

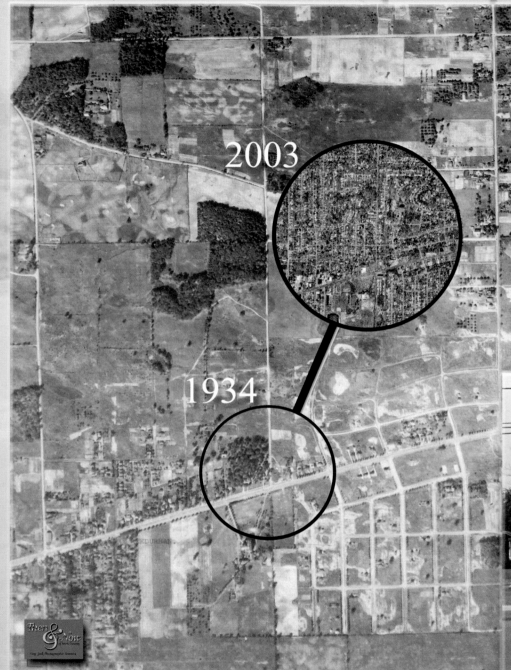

2003

1934

1922 Perry Township map

Richville Rd. looking east at Navarre Rd. Class reunion being led into town by local band.

Improved junction of Perry Rd. and 12th St. N.W.

Brader Print of the Prospect Hill Fruit Farm and residence of L. Stump. in the mid 1800's.
The Stump Home today.

PIKE TOWNSHIP

After first being a part of Canton Township, Pike Township was organized in 1815. The earliest known settler in Pike was George Young. Of German background, he and his family settled near the center of the township, where they farmed. By 1811 he had accumulated cash to purchase a quarter section and built a log cabin. He later built the township's first brick house, at the corner of Downing and Bridge streets. It is believed that Young was drafted three times during the War of 1812, but each time he paid $100 to have a substitute fight for him. From his two marriages, Young fathered 19 children. By 1938 his descendants numbered 800. 1811 saw the arrival of Jonathan Cable, who planted the first five acres of wheat. His land became the site of the U. S. Quarry Tile Company.

The first township election was held in 1815 in the home of Henry Bordner. Mr. Bordner and Phillip Seffert became township officers in the election. Oinney Guest, who arrived in 1812 with his father-in-law Benjamin Miller, was elected the first justice of peace to serve the township. Guest, an ordained Baptist minister, performed many of the weddings in the area.

The village water well at Main Ave and Walnut St. The brick structure was added in the late 1920's.

Ralph and Grace Lupher home, circa 1942. Larry Bowling restored and remodeled this house and resides here.

The Cook Farm on Maplehurst Ave., circa 1910. The farm has been owned by the Cook family for 100 years.

125

The Farber farm house on Farber Road.

The East Sparta Grade School on Poplar St., circa 1911.

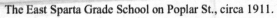

The Baltimore and Ohio Railroad Station in East Sparta, circa 1906.

Birdseye view of Walnut St. looking west and showing the grist mill on Nimishellen Creek circa 1903.

Green Ridge School house and cemetery on Greenhill Cabin Road.

The past and present entrance to the United States Ceramic Tile Company. Cliff Brown is setting at the past entrance.

The Heinbuck barn that sat between State Rt. 800 and East Sparta Ave at Battlesburg Rd.

The Grist Mill on the West Bank of the Nimishellen at Walnut St. Built by Michael Conrad in 1903.

Former Buckman Ford Dealership. Now Williams Toyota Lift Dealership.

War Memorial in East Sparta Cemetery.

Pike Grange #1669. circa 1935. The group was organized in 1907.

Hacketts Gulf Station and Resturant at Westbrook St. S.E. and State Rt. 800. Now owned by Bob and Betty Board.

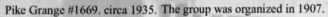

East Sparta Christian Church on Main Ave., circa 1948.

Asbury United Methodist Church on Ridge Ave. at Battlesburg., circa 1934-35.

The Baum Farm on State Rt. 800, circa 1915.

East Sparta Methodist Church on Pine St., circa 1940.

Main Ave. formerly Buffalo St., looking south. circa 1900.

Melscheimer Church and cemetery on Ridge Ave., circa 1960. The original Church Bell is shown. The church was torn down in 1960.

Past and present township school transportation.

Originally the Nolan Walker Confectionery and Barber Shop, this was also known as the Colonial Building, St. Cloud Hotel and Black's Confectionery and Barber Shop. Known the most as J & J Grill. Now Town Pump Bar.

Carnahan Brothers Groceries and Meats. Now an apartment building on Main Ave.

Truax's Blacksmith Shop. Corner of Chestnut Ave and Walnut St., circa 1900.

PLAIN TOWNSHIP

One of the five original townships created with the organization of Stark County in 1809, Plain Township included the present Lake, Lawrance, and Jackson township areas, as well as that of Green and Franklin townships in Summit County. The name, Plain, aptly describes the gentle rolling terrain of the area. The territory was sparsely settled and was inhabited by wild animals.

The first two families to build log cabins there in 1805 were those of Henry Friday, a Hessian mercenary, and Irishman Hugh Cunningham. Several others migerated from Pennsylvania during the next three years, including George Harter, with his family of seven.
The Harter home was the site of the first elections to be held in the township.

George Adam Rex built the first mill in the township in 1811. Abraham Holm and his son, Jacob, opened a store next to the mill and also operated a tannery.

Johannes Staunch started the Holy Trinity Lutheran Church in 1806 in the cabin of Jacob Loutzenheiser (reportedly the third cabin built in the township). The predominant religious faith of the early settlers was Lutheran and German Reformed. These congregation joined to erect a log church, where worship services were alternated between the two faiths. Services were conducted in German until 1835, when English was accepted as part of the worship service.

The township has one of the oldest cemeteries in the county, Henry Warstler cemetery, in continuous operation since 1808.

Much of the township was already occupied by 1815 and the community boasted of four public schools, a private school and a German - language school. It was this Pennsylvania German ancestry that was reflected in the choice of New Berlin as the name of the community platted in 1831 by Samuel Bachtel.

Walker's Mountain, located on the southeast corner of I-77 and Everhard Road.

William H. Martin's single wing airplane. He could not afford to have a motor built , so test flights were made by having it towed by horses or auto. The Smithsonian Institution had it hung by the Spirit of St. Louis.

The cement plant in Middlebranch was started by Zebulon Davis, as Diamond Portland Cement, which is now owned by Essrock Industries.

The Middlebranch School has served as a high school, elementary, and now a middle school.

Lakeside Country Club was located at the north end of Meyers Lake. It had nine holes, located on the parcel called Shrine Village.

Jacob Bair arrived in Ohio 1805 and built this home in 1846. It is located on Applegrove Rd. east of Market Ave.

The Jacob Bair Home built in 1867, currently owned by the Charles Homer Family.

Cocklin's home across the street from the general store in Middlebranch.

The Oval City Mill located at the corner of Werner Church Rd. and Middlebranch Rd. Photo at lower right shows where the water race came in to drive the Mill wheel. It is still open at the arrow.

Most villages of Stark County had rail service. Middlebranch Station was located at the end of Depot Street.

The Cocklin General Store was on this vacant lot. It supplied the local area with food as well as hardware.

Looking north on Market St. (now Middlebranch Rd.) A vacant sits where the Cocklin General Store stood.

In the early 1900s there were two villages, Middlebranch and Oval City. This is Oval City's Washington Hall School redesigned as a residence.

The old post office was on the same piece of ground as this white building.

This cornfield was the location of the well known Poison Ivy Barn. Many young people came home itching after working near it.

The Firestone farm has been subdivided to make this residential area across the street from the Oakwood Golf Course.

Looking north on Main St. (Middlebranch Rd.) in the early 1900's at the intersection of Diamond St.

George Wade of Pioneer Meats was married to a Firestone. They lived on this farm.

Franklin Hall School, 55th St. at Harmont Ave. NE.

George L. and Leto Firestone-Wade Farm barn.

The Smith farm on Schneider Rd. west of Middlebranch Rd. is now the new site of the Glenoak High School.

Middlebranch Hardware, circa 1955, and today.

The Little Flower Church once stood on this vacant lot.

The John A. Fohl Farm has been broken up into lots and now has large homes.

136

SANDY TOWNSHIP

Named for its productive sandy soil, Sandy Township was established on March 16, 1809. At the time of the early settlers, there were a few Indian and horse trails through the wilderness, notably the Tuscarawas Indian trail down the Sandy Creek and pioneer trails from Steubenville to Canton and Bethlehem.

The first stage coach line from Canton to Steubenville, operated by Bezaleel Wells, went through Sandy Township. Later, John Brown developed a three-foot gauge one-half mile railroad through the township. The embankment, bridges, trestle works, and rails were made of maple flattened with wooden pins. Mules powered the system, which was used to transport stone from David Reed Stone Quarry to Elson's dam.

Settlers moving into the area between 1808 and 1810 included the William Knots family (whose farm was the location of the first schoolhouse), James Reeves, the Downing family, the William Thompson family, the Peter Mottice family, John Reed, Isaac Van Meter, and John Hewitt among others. Attorneys Charles W. Sickafoose and Harvey Creighton are descended from early families who had adjoining farms in the township.

The Elson Flour Mill, built in 1834, in Magnolia and as it looks today.

Tozzi's Restaurant, built around 1925, in Magnolia, and as it appears today

The A. R. Elson Home, built in 1879, is a landmark in these parts, today it is Elson Bed and Breakfast in Magnolia.

Richard Elson Greer Home, built in 1910; In 1929, it became the McCreery Funeral Home in Magnolia, which today is the Finefrock Funeral Home.

The Evangelical United Brethren Church built in 1874 once stood here. In 1985, the Frank and Chey Schubert family built this log cabin where they reside today.

The Trinity Lutheran Church of Magnolia, built in 1905, with the lowering of the bell-tower, and as it looks today.

The Mohawk Theater had a rich past, built in the early 1900's, As Cibo's Restaurant it has kept this tradition alive as the area's finest restaurant.

The Sandy and Beaver Canal, built 1845-49; with 1937 photo and as it looks today.

The Kloppman Tin Shop, established 1882 in Magnolia. Today it is an antique shop and apartments.

Waynesburg Carriage Company, established in 1894, continues in business as an automobile dealership.

Magnolia School, built in 1896, is now Magnolia Village Hall.

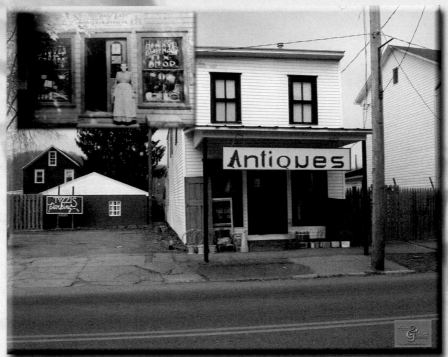

N. Main St. in Waynesburg. The large building has been a shoe store, Gruber's Pool Room, and Tozzi and Prati Grocery Store. The next building to the left was Stemple's Confectionery. Today it's an empty lot.

Beans and Elsass Dry Goods in the early 1900's, Today Philip Elsass Store and Apartment Building.

Waynesburg S. Main St., where Ernest Youman Shoe Store and Yvo Weisburn Appliance Store were located. Later, the building housed Downes Nationwide Insurance Agency and is the Nationwide Insurance and Financial Services Building.

The Baltimore and Ohio Railroad Station of Magnolia in the early 1900's, the railroad station was relocated behind the Magnolia Mill, today the Village Park.

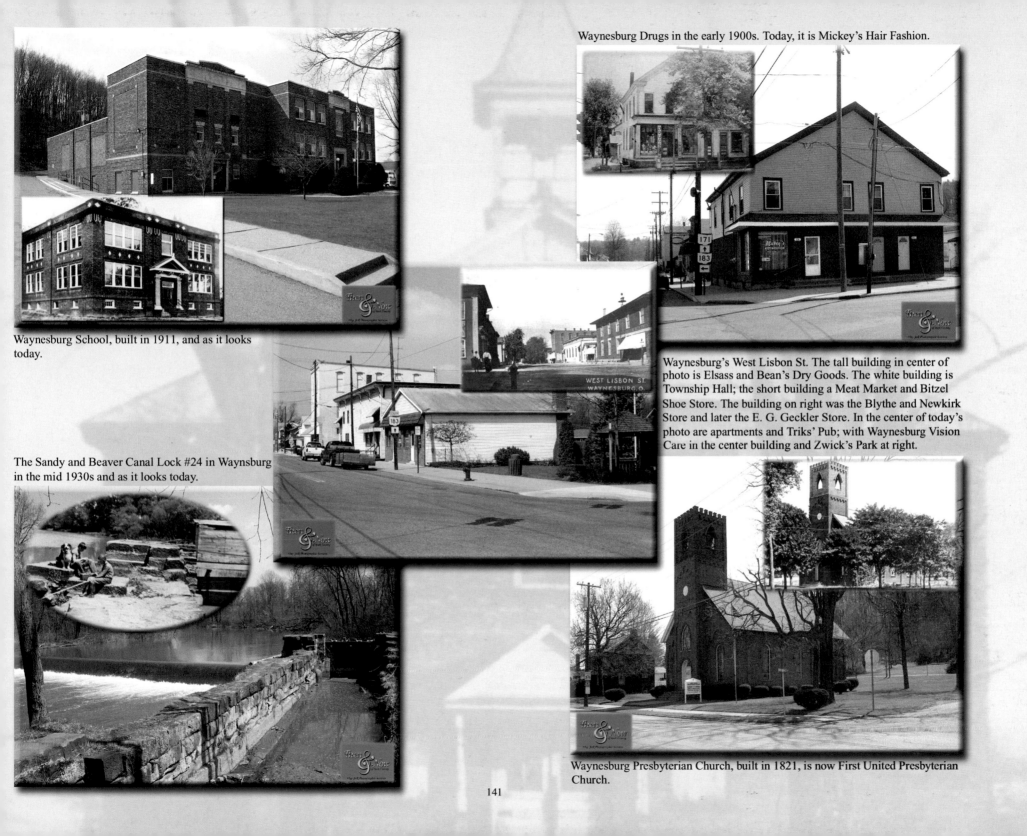

Waynesburg Drugs in the early 1900s. Today, it is Mickey's Hair Fashion.

Waynesburg School, built in 1911, and as it looks today.

The Sandy and Beaver Canal Lock #24 in Waynsburg in the mid 1930s and as it looks today.

Waynesburg's West Lisbon St. The tall building in center of photo is Elsass and Bean's Dry Goods. The white building is Township Hall; the short building a Meat Market and Bitzel Shoe Store. The building on right was the Blythe and Newkirk Store and later the E. G. Geckler Store. In the center of today's photo are apartments and Triks' Pub; with Waynesburg Vision Care in the center building and Zwick's Park at right.

Waynesburg Presbyterian Church, built in 1821, is now First United Presbyterian Church.

Waynesburg Carriage in the 1920's, and as it appears today

The Hamilton House stood here on S.Main St. in Waynesburg. Now a private residence.

High St. looking east in Magnolia with school on left. Today Village Hall and Fire Dept. and Historical Society.

Canal St. and North Main St. looking south in Magnolia

SUGARCREEK TOWNSHIP

The new township formed from part of Tuscarawas Township in 1816 took its name from the Sugar Creek which runs through that section of the county (the creek was named for the sugar maples that were abundant when early settlers arrived). Jacob Grounds, who came in 1808, is said to be the first settler in this southern township. Henry Willard built a grist mill along the creek in 1816; Henry Corninger started a distillery just a half-mile north of the mill. The latest and slowest township to be settled and the last township to lay out a village, Sugar Creek Township gave birth to four communities; Justus Station, Plainsburg (first called Stambaughtown), Beach City (origianlly Willard's Mill), and Wilmot. Two early churchs serving these communities were the Weimer United Brethern Church, built in 1825, and the Bunker Hill Methodist Episcopal Church, built circa 1830.

The township was known for residents with push and pull and during the Civil War, the township sent more soldiers to the Union Army, in proportion to its population, than any other township in the United States.

Early Shearer's Foods Distribution warehouse. They have moved to Brewster with manufacturing and distribution at one location.

The first grist mill as built in 1816 in Sugarcreek. The inset shows employees of the Duncan Elevator Company in 1929. The site is currently an antique and gift shop.

Wilmot School was built in 1840. When dismantled, it supplied the foundation for this home.

Early photos of the Brewster Cheese Factory and today to show how it has grown.

Public school of Justus was located on this property. The middle school will soon take this place.

The General Store from 1900 is now the location of Mulheim & Son Handcrafted Country & Shaker Furniture.

Looking north on the public square in downtown Brewster.

The Klingle Farm is now the location of Fairless High School.

Wetzel Ice Cream was an early restaurant-tavern. Now it houses the Amvets.

Brewster Main St. looking northeast from the square.

Early Sugarcreek Twp. School, now used as a meeting place for the township trustees.

Main St. looking west in Beach City.

Looking west on Route 250, showing the quiet shopping area.

The Wheeling & Lake Erie turntable with a steam locomotive, today the locomotives are powered by diesel engines.

You have to stop and smell the roses, if you do you will begin to enjoy the homeiness of the quiet country.

The Beach City passenger station has been removed and replaced by a storage area for rail repairs.

This spot in Beach City has had a colorful life. The home of the "Wonderful New Process Vapor Stoves," Lawrence Grocery, and a laudromat were erased by fire and not replaced.

Boxers General Store and Post Office in Justus. This was the place for the young to get penny sweets and Ice Cream.

Downtown section of Beach City looking west toward the Village Hall.

From the square looking northwes is the Beckett Candy building. Beckett was known for the best Orientals in this part of Ohio.

First named the Brewster Railroad YMCA to provide housing for railroad men, it became the Wandle House. It was constructed in 1916. Since then the building has restaurants, a movie theater, a bowling alleys, and the headquarters for the Historical Society of Sugarcreek Township.

Bremkamp's Service Station stood here. The attendant would work in the garden until someone would pullup and ask for gas to go to town at 17 cents per gallon.

Beach City had its spots for local talk and refreshment. This is one of the early places. Later it was a Barber Shop, and is now the residence of Marylou Hanlen.

Built in the early 1900s and occupied by a Tinsmith for many years. It is now a beauty shop.

Falls House Stagecoach stop and hotel until 1936 was the place to enjoy a weekend or just meet friends. Several Presidents including McKinley enjoyed its hospitality. The stone from this building was purchased by Dr. Clovis and brought to Canton where an architect was commissioned to design this new home on N. Market Ave.

TUSCARAWAS TOWNSHIP

Tuscarawas Township was organized in March of 1810 on land purchased from the Indians by the Treaty of Fort Industry on July 4, 1805. William Dean came from Pennsylvania in 1809 to settle in the area. A year later there were 145 residents, basically representing three groups: Pennslyvania Dutch, the New Yorkers, and the Scotch-Irish Presbyterians.

The township was reduced to its present limits by 1816 when portions were taken for Jackson, Lawrence, Perry, Bethlehem, and Sugarcreek townships in Stark County, and Franklin Township in Summit County.

The first justice of the peace was William Henry, who had come to the area in 1807 to help survey the township. Henry, who also operated a general store, built the toll bridge across the Tuscarawas River for State Road and helped found Wooster. The township has the county's westernmost community, East Greenville, which was platted in 1829 by Rev. Jacob Frey. While it is the only Stark County community to be recorded by an ordained minister, East Greenville became known as a rough and tumble community because of the coal miners who moved into the town. Much of the township is still farmland. The major industry is the Massillon Refractories, opened in 1919, to manufacture insulating (fire) brick.

The Methodist Episcopal Church, East Greenville.

The public school in East Greenville, now a used car dealership.

East. Greenville Menorial Day Parade, 1913, Note that the house remains standing with little change.

The Pocock Mine.

Pocock Mine,
E. Greenville O.

2003

1934

Aerial photo of E. Greenville

Aerial view of the village of Sippo

2003

1934

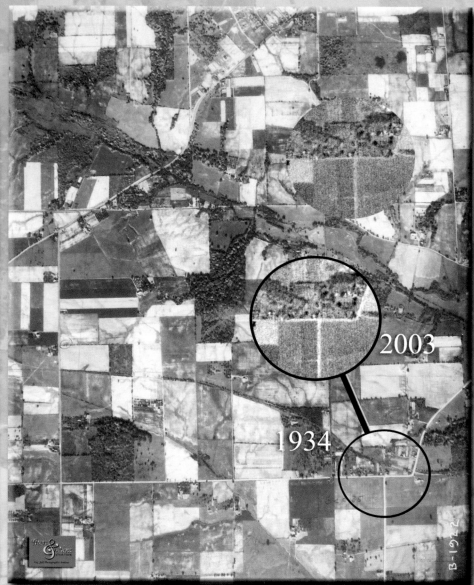

2003

1934

Aerial view of the village of Pigeon Run.

Dublin School on Wooster St.

Aerial view of the village of Stanwood

2003

1934

The Stanberry School built in 1829

1915 Class Reunion Stanwood School

1947 Stanwood School class time out, Built in 1879, located on the corner of Alabama and Stanwood

WASHINGTON TOWNSHIP

Washington Township, on the eastern side of Stark County, was founded in 1820 when the area seperated from Lexington Twp. At that time it was a heavily wooded area with many small creeks. Four towns were platted but only two survived. In there early days Freeburg and Maximo were bustling little towns. Freeburg cosists mostly of private residences at this time; however, Maximo still has a post office, small grocery store and the railroad going through the town daily. The township still has many farms and there are businesses and churches scattered throughout. The elementary school is the only educational building and is located across from the volunteer fire department which has protected the township for more than 50 years.

F.A. Brader, an itinerant artist drew this picture of the Bischel Farm on Union Ave. There is still a farm there; however time has changed it from its appearance in the late 1800s

The public school in Maximo hosted all the other schools in the township to a picnic. This photo taken in the early 1900's shows the weather did not always cooperate. Now the Maximo Zion Church use the land the school sat on for there own picnics in the pavilion.

Another hand-drawn farm scene by F.A. Brader shows a farm on Kenmore St. in the 1870s. The farm is still there with several newer buildings added.

155

If you wanted fresh-squeezed cider, you traveled to Schmucker's Cider Mill on the corner of Louisville St. & Paris Ave. Now if you go to this same location you will find Motts Greenhouse and Bulk Food Service.

The community of Freeburg as seen from the air around 1950 has changed some if you look at the same view, taken in 2003.

Maximo's Railroad Station was a busy place in 1890. It was located east of the St. Joseph's Catholic Cemetery. As train travel diminished, the train station was no longer a necessity, so the structure is now vacant.

Charles Burns's General Store in Maximo sold anything that anyone would have needed, from horse collars to penny candy. The store was a landmark in the township for years. A fire destroyed this friendly gathering place, and eventually a private home was built there.

A favorite hangout for the locals was Les Egli's Service Station which was across Beechwood Ave. from the Johnson farm. With the changing of the road Les's became a menory and the BP station took it's place.

The corner of Beechwood Ave. and State Rt. 62 was the home and farm of Fred Johnson and family. The buildings are gone now, the bank removed, and Beechwood Ave. was rerouted to meet Sawburg Rd. Wally Armor's car lot now sits on the corner.

The Honaker farm, which joined Job Scott's farm, was located on the corner of Oakhill Ave. and State Rt. 62. It met the same fate as Job's and was replaced by Wal-Mart.

Job Scott raised and supported his family on this farm on State Rt. 62. Only going to the store for the barest of necessities, he would not have imagined a mall full of stores to be set on his farmland.

The Catholics of Maximo and surrounding area attended church in the original St. Joseph's Church, which sat next to the nuns' residence on Oakhill Ave. When their new church was built the old building was torn down, and is now a vacant lot covered with grass.

Family reunions were always fun when you went to Grandma & Grandpa's as this picture shows of the Culler Reunion. Sam Ruff moved this house from Freeburg c. 1875. In 1916 his daughter Laura's husband Henry removed one-half of the house, then moved the half back to this location for their family reunion.

The Fairmount Children's Home was built in 1877 for Stark and Columbiana counties. The inset, taken in the 1920s, displays the entire structure. The color photo shows the remains of the home, which was destroyed by fire in 2002.

The Freeburg Church of the Brethern shown in the c. 1945 picture used seperate doors for men and women to enter and sit in the church. By 1960 they remodeled. No longer practicing this tradition, they bricked up the doors and moved the entranceway to the end of the church.